Also by Tom Cooper in the Africa@War series:
Great Lakes Conflagration: The Second Congo War, 1998–2003 (Volume XIV)

Co-published in 2013 by:

Helion & Company Limited
26 Willow Road
Solihull
West Midlands
B91 1UE
England
Tel. 0121 705 3393
Fax 0121 711 4075
email: info@helion.co.uk
website: www.helion.co.uk

and

30° South Publishers (Pty) Ltd.
16 Ivy Road
Pinetown 3610
South Africa
email: info@30degreessouth.co.za
website: www.30degreessouth.co.za

Text © Tom Cooper, 2013
Colour profiles © Tom Cooper, 2013
Maps and other colour illustrations ©
    Tamara Zeller & Pia Dworzak or as
    individually credited

Designed & typeset by SA Publishing
    Services (kerrincocks@gmail.com)
Cover design by Kerrrin Cocks

Printed for Helion & Co by Henry Ling Ltd.,
    Dorchester, Dorset and for
    30° South Publishers by Pinetown
    Printers, Durban, South Africa

SA ISBN 978-1-920143-83-1
UK ISBN 978-1-909384-65-1

British Library Cataloguing-in-Publication
    Data
A catalogue record for this book is
    available from the British Library

Front cover: Over one million Rwandans, primarily Hutus, fled to eastern Zaire during 1994–96, where thousands died of malnutrition, exhaustion and epidemics, even before some of their camps came under the control of Hutu extremists. This photograph shows an FAZ truck, with soldiers onboard, passing the bodies of refugees who have died of cholera in the camps in the Goma area, July 1994. *Photo unmultimedia.org*

CONTENTS

Note: In order to simplify the use of this book, all names, locations and geographic designations are as provided in *The Times World Atlas*, or other traditionally accepted major sources of reference, as of the time of described events. Correspondingly, the term 'Congo' designates the area of the former Belgian colony of the Congo Free State, granted independence as the Democratic Republic of the Congo in June 1960 and in use until 1971 when the country was renamed Republic of Zaire, which, in turn, reverted to Democratic Republic of the Congo in 1997, and which remains in use today. As such, Congo is not to be mistaken for the former French colony of Middle Congo (Moyen Congo), officially named the Republic of the Congo on its independence in August 1960, also known as Congo-Brazzaville.

Abbreviations

4WD	four-wheel drive
AA	anti-aircraft
AAA	anti-aircraft artillery
AB	Agusta-Bell (Italian–American helicopter manufacturers)
AdA	*Armée de l'Air* (French Air Force)
ADCC	Air Defence Consultants Corporation (Israeli commercial military enterprise)
ADF	Allied Democratic Forces/Front (armed opposition group in Uganda since 1990s)
AFB	Air Force Base
AFDL	*Alliance des Forces Démocratiques pour la Libération du Congo* (Alliance of Democratic Forces for the Liberation of Congo-Zaire, Rwandan-supported insurgent organization in Zaire, 1996–97)
AK-47	*Automat Kalashnikova* (former Soviet or Eastern Bloc-manufactured 7.62mm assault rifle)
AML	*Automitrailleuse Légère* (French-manufactured Panhard scout car and armoured vehicle)
An	Antonov (design bureau led by Oleg Antonov)
ANC	*Armée Nationale Congolaise* (Congolese National Army, 1960–71)
APC	armoured personnel carrier
AT-14	ASCC, codename for Vikhr, Soviet-/Russian-made ATGM
ATGM	anti-tank guided missile
BAC	British Aircraft Corporation
BAe	British Aerospace
CAP	combat air patrol
CAS	close air support
CASA	*Construcciones Aeronáuticas SA* (Spanish aircraft manufacturer)
CBU	cluster bomb unit
CIA	Central Intelligence Agency (USA)
C-in-C	commander-in-chief
c/n	construction number
CO	commanding officer
DoD	Department of Defence (USA)
DSP	*Division Special Présidentielle* (Special Presidential Division FAZ)
ECM	electronic countermeasures
ELINT	electronic intelligence
ENI	*Ente Nazionale Idrocarburi* (Italian state-owned petroleum company)
EO	Executive Outcomes (South African commercial military enterprise)
FAA	*Forças Armadas Angolanas* (Angolan military since 1992)
FANA	*Força Aérea Nacional* (Angolan Air Force, since 1992)
FAR	*Forces Armées Rwandaise* (Rwandan Armed Forces, 1962–94)
FAZ	*Forces Armées Zaïroise* (Zairian Army, 1971–1996)
FAZA	*Force Aérienne Zaïroise* (Zairian Air Force, 1971–96)
FDD	*Forces pour la Défense de la Démocratie* (Forces for the Defence of Democracy, armed opposition group in Burundi, 1990s/2000s)
FIM-92A	US-made MANPADS (full designation FIM-92A Stinger)
FNLA	*Frente Nacional de Libertacao de Angola* (National Front for the Liberation of Angola, armed group opposing Portuguese rule in Angola 1960–75, later fighting against the MPLA government in 1970s/80s)
FNLC	*Front National pour la Libération du Congo* (National Front for the Liberation of the Congo, insurgent organization in Zaire/Congo, 1990s)
GCI	ground controlled interception
GP	general-purpose (bomb)
HE	high explosive
HQ	headquarters
IAI	Israeli Aircraft Industries (since 2006 Israeli Aerospace Industries)
IAP	international airport
IDF	Israeli Defence Forces
IFF	identification friend or foe
IFV	infantry fighting vehicle
IP	instructor pilot
IR	infrared, electromagnetic radiation, longer than deepest red light sensed as heat
Il	Ilyushin (the design bureau led by Sergey Vladimirovich Ilyushin, also known as OKB-39)
km	kilometre
LRA	Lord's Resistance Army (armed opposition group in Uganda)
MAGRIVI	*Mutuelle des Agriculteurs des Virunga* (Famers' Society of Virunga)
MANPADS	Man-Portable Air Defence System(s) (light surface-to-air missile system that can be carried and deployed in combat by a single soldier
MBT	main battle tank
MHz	megahertz, millions of cycles per second
Mi	Mil (Soviet/Russian helicopter designer and manufacturer)
MiG	*Mikoyan i Gurevich* (the design bureau led by Artyom Ivanovich Mikoyan and Mikhail Iosifovich Gurevich, also known as OKB-155 or MMZ 'Zenit')
MILAN	*Missile d'infanterie léger antichar* (French-made ATGM)
MoD	Ministry of Defence
MPLA	*Movimento Popular de Libertação de Angola* (People's Movement for the Liberation of Angola, leftist anti-colonial movement in Angola during the 1960s and 1970s; later ruling party of Angola)
MPR	*Mouvement Populaire de la Révoultion* (Popular Movement of the Revolution, Mobutu's political party)
NAF	Namibian Air Force (formerly the Namibian Defence Force/Air Wing)
Nav/attack	used for navigation and to aim weapons against surface targets
NCO	non-commissioned officer

NDF/AW	Namibian Defence Force/Air Wing
NL	*Namibiese Lugmag* (Afrikaans for the unofficial designation often used for Namibian Air Force in everyday communication)
NRA	National Resistance Army (insurgent organization in Uganda, 1981–85)
OAU	Organization of African Unity
OCU	operational conversion unit
ORBAT	order of battle
PMC	private military company
PRP	People's Revolutionary Party (insurgent organization in Zaire, 1980s)
RAF	Royal Air Force
RPA	Rwandan Patriotic Army (military wing of the RPF, 1987–94, and official designation of the Rwandan military, 1994–2002)
RDF	Rwanda Defence Force (official designation since 2002)
RDF/AF	Rwanda Defence Force/Air Force
RPF	Rwandan Patriotic Front (insurgent organization in Uganda and Rwanda, 1987–94)
RHAW	radar homing and warning system
RWR	radar warning receiver
SA-2 Guideline	ASCC, codename for S-75 Dvina, Soviet SAM system
SA-6 Gainful	ASCC, codename for ZRK-SD Kub/Kvadrat, Soviet SAM system
SA-7 Grail	ASCC, codename for 9K32 Strela-2, Soviet MANPADS

SA-14 Gremlin	ASCC, codename for 9M36 Strela-3, Soviet MANPADS
SA-16 Gimlet	ASCC, codename for 9M313 Igla-1, Soviet MANPADS
SAM	surface-to-air missile
SADC	Southern African Development Community
SAM	surface-to-air missile
SARM	*Service d'Action et de Renseignement Militaire* (Zairian Military Intelligence Bureau)
SNIP	*Service National d'Intelligence et Protection* (National Service for Intelligence and Protection, top Zairian intelligence agency)
Su	Sukhoi (the design bureau led by Pavel Ossipowich Sukhoi, also known as OKB-51)
TAM	Tbilisi Aerospace Manufacturing (Georgian aircraft manufacturing company)
TASA	Tbilisi Aircraft State Association (Georgian aircraft manufacturing company)
UHF	ultra-high frequency
UNHCR	UN High Commissioner for Refugees
UNITA	*Uniao Nacional para a Independència Total de Angola* (National Union for the Total Independence of Angola, armed group opposing Portuguese rule in the 1960s and 1970s, then opposing the MPLA until 2003)
UNRWA	United Nations Relief and Works Agency
UPDF	Uganda People's Defence Force
USAF	United States Air Force
VHF	very high frequency

CHAPTER ONE:
BACKGROUND

The First and Second Congo wars, 1996–97 and 1998–2003 respectively, were caused by a variety of geopolitical factors that can be found in a labyrinth of domestic problems, such as ethnic, political and economic relations, added to questionable dictatorships, endemic corruption and nepotism. The impact of direct and indirect involvement of foreign interests and business connections, arms trafficking, money laundering and other organized crime, all too had roles to play. For an average Western observer, none of these might appear sufficiently serious to justify the immense tragedy that befell the country that is today the Democratic Republic of Congo (DRC), or neighbouring Rwanda, where the two wars described in these volumes actually began. However, under closer scrutiny, it becomes obvious that these wars were primarily driven by greed, to control and exploit the immense mineral and natural resources of the Congo. Tragically, these wars were exploited by various extremists, to the degree that, according to various UN reports, some 3.8 million – some sources put the figure as high as 5.4 million – people died. Combined, these wars were therefore the third-most deadliest conflicts of the 20th century, after the two World Wars.

This tragedy has not been underreported. Plenty of information has been published over the years but, until recently, many publications have proved to be smokescreens, actually designed to censor, manipulate and cover up the real story, keeping events well away from the mainstream media, and thus the public. In light of reports of widespread suffering and the perfidy of the players who influenced these conflicts, most related publications that became available concentrated on unravelling and describing the political aspects. Military-related studies are scarce and limited.

The commonly accepted *raison d'être* of the First and Second Congo wars appears simple enough. In 1994, age-old tensions between the ethnic groups of Hutus and Tutsis in Rwanda spun out of control, resulting in the murder of a million Tutsis and moderate Hutus. Twenty per cent of the Rwandan population was slaughtered. Due to the flight of Rwandan Hutus to the Congo, the conflict then spilled across the border, prompting the war that is the topic of this book. The Congo is a country that has experienced countless insurgencies and much destabilization since its independence in 1960. The government in Kinshasa, the country's capital, has long been at odds with indigenous Tutsis, and those 'imported' as forced labour by the Belgian colonial authorities in the 1920s. The arrival of a horde of Hutu refugees – among them the extremists responsible for the 1994 genocide agitating for a counterattack on the new, Tutsi-controlled government in Rwanda – prompted the Tutsis to support various local militias in an uprising that eventually resulted in all-out war against the central government in Kinshasa. Ultimately, the rebels won and the First Congo War ended in May 1997, but as soon as the new government took power, it turned against its former allies, prompting mutinies in the Congolese military, another rebellion and fresh intervention by Rwanda, followed by Uganda and Burundi, in August and September 1998. Under threat of being overrun, the government in Kinshasa then requested help from its allies in the Southern African Development Community (SADC), which had been the first to recognize it internationally. Angola, Namibia and Zimbabwe replied positively, and deployed significant contingents of their armed forces. Amid much chaos and severe fighting across the country and, 'with some foreign support', the rebels should have managed to defeat the SADC forces and put more than half the country under their control, before a series of negotiations, between 1999 and 2001, coupled with international pressure and the high costs of the war, ultimately forced all foreign troops to withdraw. The Second Congo War thus came to an end in 2003, but internal unrest, uprisings and mutinies continue to this day.

This is the commonly accepted version. But, as the latest in-depth studies of the geopolitical factors that led to this war have shown, the situation was anything but this simple. Although the exact reasons and processes of the Rwandan genocide appear to have been properly investigated, the government that installed itself in Kigali in 1994 is facing increased and documented accusations of applying similar genocidal practices in their pursuit of Hutu refugees inside its borders and through the eastern Congo, while forcing survivors to return to Rwanda during 1996/97. Furthermore, Kigali, as well as the governments of Uganda and Burundi, through their top military commanders, but more so the governments of Angola and Zimbabwe, appear to have exploited the Second War, by exercising political influence in Kinshasa, to plunder Congolese mineral wealth, pocketing billions in the process. Perhaps, most importantly though, is that the post-genocidal Rwandan government maintained, and still maintains, very close connections with top political and business establishments in the USA and Israel. These relationships enabled it to build up its military strength and launch two campaigns of fairly strategic proportion, the first resulting in the conquest of the entire Congo in 1996/97; the second campaign was stopped only with help of SADC military intervention in 1998–2001.

Under such circumstances, it is not surprising that details of the military campaigns launched during the course of these two wars remain obfuscated.

A labyrinth of rivers and mountains

Although often neglected in published studies, local terrain and climatic circumstances continue to dictate even modern warfare. In order to enable a better understanding of how and why specific military operations were undertaken in the fashion in which they occurred, and how they became possible, it is necessary to take at least a brief look at the country, its natural resources, historical, political and ethnic relations, and the neighbouring countries that became involved.

The Congo is the second-largest country in Africa, after Algeria. It is four times the size of France, or comparable in size to either the entire Western Europe or the United States east of the Mississippi River. Situated in Central Africa, the country encompasses a vast depression, constituting its central area, which is surrounded by plateaux and mountains, all covered with dense vegetation. The area is practically encircled by the mighty Congo River – the second longest river in Africa and the seventh longest in the world – and its hundreds of tributaries within the Congo Basin. Formed on the Katanga plateau in southeastern Congo, the river flows north and is navigable as far as the city of Kisangani where the Stanley Falls (now Boyoma Falls), a series of wide cataracts, impedes navigation. Downstream from this point the river is navigable again and arcs west and then south to Kinshasa (formerly Leopoldville), forming the northern boundary with the Central African Republic and a portion of the country's western boundary with the Republic of the Congo. The river and its tributaries provide a vast network of navigable waterways and have great – yet little used – hydroelectric potential. Hydroelectric plants produce virtually all the energy the country needs (the major hydroelectric plant at Inga, on the Lower Congo, could actually produce 15 times the amount of electricity required by the country).

On its lower course, the Congo widens to form a lake, or Malebo Pool (formerly Stanley Pool), on the southern side of which is the capital Kinshasa, while Brazzaville, capital of the neighbouring Republic of the Congo, sits on the northern bank. Even more water can be found in the east of the Congo where a number of lakes, important for transportation and fishing, mark many of its borders, including Lake Albert and Lake Edward which it shares with Uganda, Lake Kivu on the border with Rwanda, Lake Tanganyika (the seventh largest in the world) forming the entire border with Tanzania and much of Burundi, and Lake Mweru straddling the Zambian border. The area along these lakes is dominated by the Ruwenzori Range in the northeast, which contains the Congo's highest point, Margherita Peak (5,109m). In the east there are the Virunga Mountains that include eight active volcanoes. The southern part of the country is dominated by dry grassland interspersed with trees, fringed by the rugged Katanga plateau, about 1,000m above sea level.

The country's climate is very hot and humid, with average annual temperatures in the low central area of 27°C, reaching highs well above 40°C during February. Frequent heavy rains occur from April to November north of the equator and from October through May south of the equator.

Natural resources

The Congo is immensely rich in natural resources and boasts some of the biggest mineral deposits in the world. According to various estimates, the county should have up to US$24 trillions' worth of untapped deposits of raw mineral ores. These include the world's largest reserves of cobalt and columbite-tantalite (better known as coltan, an ore containing two metals, niobium and tantalum), and some of the largest reserves of diamonds, gold, silver, copper, uranium, tin, tungsten, zinc, manganese and cadmium.

Gold was found by the Belgians in the Kilo-Moto area in 1906, followed by copper, cobalt and uranium, all discovered between 1911 and 1932; until today no less than 82 specific minerals – foremostly various heavy metals much sought after by modern, high-end technology industries – were found and described for the first time in the Congo. Congolese uranium was used in the nuclear bombs that the USA dropped on Japan in 1945, while its massive coltan reserves are crucial for worldwide production of everyday electronic devices, like cell phones. Offshore oil reserves have been drilled since the mid-1970s and some exploitation is taking place but, according to

Prince Leopold mine, as seen in 1944. *Photo UMHK*

The huge cobalt mine at Ruwe, as seen in the 1950s.
Photo Mark Lepko Collection

various estimates, untapped reserves are likely to further increase the potential income of the country in the future.

The worked mineral deposits are distributed over Pre-Cambrian massifs bordering to the south, east and northeast in a vast sedimentary central basin. Most minerals are present in such quantities and are so accessible that they can be mined with little capital investment. Although theoretically state-controlled, much of the mining is done by small-scale, artisanal miners who operate illegally. In addition, the area around Mbuji-May in the south-central Congo is the heartland of the country's diamond-mining industry, producing mainly industrial diamonds. Additional diamondiferous mining is exploited in Tshikapa. Large copper deposits were found in Tshiniama and Lubi, as well as in southern Shaba which is also rich in cobalt and uranium, mined in Kolwezi, Likasi, Kambowe, Shinkolobwe and Lubumbashi. The same province also contains large zinc, copper and germanium (Kipushi), tin granite (Mitwaba) and the stanniferous pegmatite (Manono) mines. In the province of Kivu there are rich tin deposits (Kalima), often accompanied by coltan that is usually found in streambeds and soft rock, but also berly, columbite and uranium (Kobokobo). The Walikale District of north Kivu is actually the centre of the highly lucrative tin-mining industry. This area is also rich in carbonatite (Lueshe), pyrochlores, and various new silicates (such as andremeyerite, combeite, götzenite and others, found especially in lava rocks along the Rwandan border).

Most of the gold is mined in the Ituri District close to Uganda, and in the Kasai-Orientale Province where the famous Kilo-Moto mine is situated. The gold is usually found deep under riverbeds or embedded in rock. Nevertheless, significant gold deposits have been found in the South Kivu region as well. Additional mineral deposits are exploited west of Kinshasa. The Lower Congo has a few deposits of zinc and lead vanadates (Kusu-Senge mine) and the Niari massif is the centre for mining copper silicates.

Although declining since the 1990s, mining continues to account for almost 90 per cent of the Congo's export earnings. A major factor when considering this decline is that most of the extraction is done in small, unregulated operations, next to no refining is undertaken inside the country and there is no regard for environmental impact assessments. Under such conditions the central government earned what was actually only a minimum in profits from extraction and exports.

Except for being rich in mineral resources, the Congo is also very rich in diverse vegetation. The country's forest reserves, covering 60

per cent of the land, are considered the most extensive in Africa. Most of the northern part of the Congo is covered with dense rainforest, and rubber trees, coffee, cotton, oil palms, banana, coconut palms and plantain are widespread – although deforestation, caused by forestry and clearing for agriculture, is an increasing environmental problem, especially in the Bas-Congo region and around Kinshasa.

Population

The extreme climatic conditions prevalent in the Congo have limited settlement and development to areas along rivers and at high altitudes, many of which have remained isolated until recently. The population consists of more than 200 ethnic groups, some 80 per cent of which are Bantu-speaking people who migrated to the area from the northwest, around 300BC. During four centuries of slave trade the Portuguese alone claimed over 13.2 million souls from the area that today makes up the DRC. Nowadays, the largest single ethnic groups are the Lunda, Luba, Kuba, Bakongo (Kongo), Mongo, Mangbetu and Azande. Pygmy groups are scattered throughout the rainforest zone, while a small number of people of European descent can primarily be found in major cities. French is the official language and principal language of business but more than 200 languages are spoken throughout the country, of which four are, principally: Ligala along the Congo River, Kikongo between Kinshasa and the coast, Swahili in the east and Tshiluba in the south. Some 72 per cent of the Congolese are nominally Christians, primarily Roman Catholic – who account for about 52 per cent of the total population. The majority of the rest adhere to traditional African beliefs but syncretic sects, which combine practices of different religions – like Kimbanguism which fuses Christian and traditional elements – have significant numbers of adherents.

The population of about 62 million people is concentrated in the eastern highlands and along rivers, with less than a third living in the cities. Except for the capital, the largest city, Kinshasa, other major urban areas are the copper-mining city of Lubumbashi (formerly Elisabethville), the south-central diamond-mining centre of Mbuji-Mayi (formerly Bakwanga), the southeastern industrial city of Kolwezi and the northeastern Congo River port of Kisangani (formerly Stanleyville). The principal seaport is Matadi, positioned on the Congo estuary, relatively close to the stretch of Atlantic which measures only 37km and forms the western border of the country.

Apart from South Africa, the Belgian Congo was the most

industrialized and developed country on the continent in 1958; 35 per cent of the all adults were in salaried employment, a ratio unknown elsewhere in Africa. Certainly, only a few thousand people were professionals, with the majority of the Congolese unqualified workers, farm labourers, petty clerks, artisans and repairmen. Still, because the Belgian paternalistic system needed disciplined, semi-qualified drones and not people who could handle responsibility, in 1960 there were only 17 university graduates out of a population of over 20 million. The situation improved marginally during the 1970s and 1980s. The government did very little for public education, remaining dependent on missionary schools founded by European and American missionaries. Primary education was (and remains) compulsory, but only around 40 per cent of school-aged children attend school, while attendance at secondary schools is only 18 per cent of those of eligible age. The nation has four universities, two in Kinshasa and one each in Lubumbashi and Kisangani, and a small number of teacher-training colleges and technical institutes.

Due to endemic corruption, nepotism, inexperience and general neglect, much of the infrastructure developed by the Belgian colonial authorities in the first half of the 20th century has deteriorated. In over 40 years of independence not a single road, railroad, hospital or school has been built. The few completed infrastructure projects – primarily related to airports – exclusively serve mining operations, bypassing towns and villages, or service the needs of local despots. The once fertile farming areas have been laid waste, producing barely enough food for those working the land. Many parts of the country are not only destabilized but practically cut off from the outside world.

Strategic problems

The region that is nowadays within the borders of the DRC was first united as the Congo Free State, a colony created by King Leopold II in the late 19th century. Renamed the Belgian Congo in 1908, it remained under Belgian rule until 1960 when it gained independence as the Republic of Congo. Ever since, the Congo has been plagued by ethnic rivalry, political instability, poverty, high crime rates, inadequate health care, high incidents of tropical disease and armed conflict. Most notably, the eastern parts of the country have never been completely free of destructive uprisings, banditry and unrest. During the 1960s the country experienced eight years of political unrest and terrible ravages of internal revolts and turmoil (see Africa@War Volume VI: Congo Unravelled), much of which was founded in a dispute for top command of the national army (Armée Nationale Congolaise, ANC) between two Congolese non-commissioned officers (NCOs) prematurely advanced to the ranks of major-general and colonel: Victor Lundula and Joseph Désiré Mobutu, respectively. The unrest was exploited by the leader of the Katanga Province, Moise Tshombe, when he declared the province's secession. This could be described as an attempt to salvage this mineral-rich area from the chaos that engulfed the rest of the country. The secession attempt and a serious armed revolt were suppressed by a four-year occupation of much of the country by a UN peacekeeping force of 15–20,000 troops.

As soon as the UN forces withdrew in 1964, the northeastern Congo erupted into leftist-led tribal warfare. Regarded as pro-communist by much of the free world, and supported by Soviet and Chinese arms, this uprising was suppressed with the help of white mercenary commandos, supported by a mercenary air force sponsored by the

View of Kinshasa and the parliament buildings, early 1960s.
Photo Marc Lepko Collection

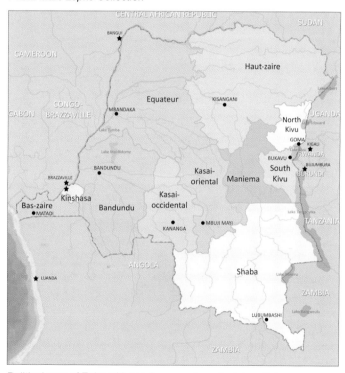

Political map of Zaire with provinces and provincial capitals.

USA, in 1965. Meanwhile, the simmering conflict between the president and prime minister reached boiling point, providing the now Lieutenant-General Mobutu with the opportunity to seize power in a coup and assume power for 'five years', which eventually became 32 years. While successfully suppressing further, if brief, revolts in 1966 and 1967, Mobutu drove into exile a number of armed opponents, including the remnants of the leftist rebels persisted with sporadic actions in eastern Congo, as well as former Katangese gendarmes who fled in 1967 when the government destroyed the growing power of their allies – the mercenary troops who had earlier helped it retain power. Although the country's long, poorly patrolled and insecure borders made it almost impossible to prevent infiltration during the

Between the mid-1960s and 1990, Mobutu was considered a staunch anti-communist and a close ally of the USA's. This photograph was taken during the early1980s and shows Mobutu (left) with the then US Secretary of Defence, Caspar Weinberger (right). *Photo US DoD*

Western side of downtown Kinshasa with the port in the background, as seen in the mid-1970s. *Photo Marc Lepko*

1970s and 1980s, the insurgents were primarily busy with the illegal extraction of natural resources, smuggling and poaching to survive. Perhaps the classic example for such a situation was the insurgency of the People's Revolutionary Party (PRP) which erupted in the south of the Kivu Province in 1967. The leader of the PRP was Laurent-Désiré Kabila, a small-time Marxist at odds with Mobutu since 1965 when, with the support of Ernesto Che Guevara, he attempted to foment a Cuban-style revolution. After the failure of this attempt, Kabila turned to smuggling gold and timber on Lake Tanganyika, before establishing the PRP and then creating a secessionist Marxist state in South Kivu, with Chinese support. This mini-state was host to collective agriculture, extortion and mineral smuggling and maintained good contacts with local Zairian military commanders who, time and again, traded military supplies in exchange for a cut of the extortion and robbery profits. Initially, the PRP resembled more of a network of loosely affiliated groups of businessmen smuggling gold and diamonds to Tanzania than a serious fighting organization. The PRP state eventually collapsed in 1987 but by this time Kabila had established himself as a wealthy businessman with excellent connections to top politicians across East Africa, many of whom were to prove influential to him and the country.

The most serious external threat to the security of Congo – namely Cuban and Soviet support for its western neighbour, Congo-Brazzaville (now the Republic of Congo) – was ameliorated, if not resolved, in 1970 by the renewal of diplomatic ties. Now secure with his power base Mobutu instigated a change of the country's name to Zaire (actually an early Portuguese transliteration of a Bantu word meaning 'big river'), while renaming himself Mobutu Sese Seko Kuku Ngbendu wa Za Banga – which means 'The all-powerful warrior who, because of his endurance and inflexible will to win, will go from conquest to conquest, leaving fire in his wake' – in 1971.

Determined to remain in power indefinitely and at any cost, Mobutu concerned himself primarily with running an increasingly and pervasively corrupt, despotic regime that mishandled the nation's resources in almost every imaginable fashion – while enjoying the wholehearted support of major powers, primarily the USA and France, as a declared bastion of anti-communism. During the Cold War, the US often used Zaire as a base and staging ground for supporting various insurgent groups supposedly fighting pro-Soviet regimes in neighbouring countries, notably Angola, in return for the provision of financial and military aid.

Chaos of democratic transition

The situation in Zaire worsened dramatically after the Cold War, shifting the equilibrium in Africa. The USA, France and Belgium practically cancelled their financial and military support for Mobutu. Although safely depositing billions in foreign accounts, the president and his closest aides showed no interest in investing this money in their own country. Similarly, although heavily dependent on the military for maintaining power, after being left without foreign financial aid, Mobutu drastically reduced the salaries of army officers, NCOs and soldiers, the latter's pay an equivalent of US$2 a month. Facing mass protest, in January 1990, he showed the first signs of being open to negotiation with his political opponents, with subsequent appointments to the government. Too far removed from the everyday realities of life in Zaire, he announced a round of 'popular consultations' and toured the country. This turned into abject humiliation as the president was entirely unprepared for the public haranguing he received from the people. Apparently drawing the lessons, he announced the advent of a democratic transition, the introduction of a multi-party system, a clear separation between party and state, a transitional government and the setting up of a commission charged with drafting a new constitution, on 24 April 1990. This transitional phase was supposed to conclude with free democratic elections at all levels.

However, Mobutu ultimately proved unwilling to implement such broad reforms. He exploited the establishment of a multi-party system to infiltrate opposition parties and provoke a series of splits from within. As a result, the National Conference – a preliminary parliament established in October 1990 – turned into a political tragicomedy, in which the opposition tore itself apart.

With the economy in tatters and the government's failure to pay state employees, demonstrations proliferated and civilian unrest began to spread through Zaire. Concentrating solely on maintaining the president and his supporters in power, the government continued exploiting the situation for its own purposes, deploying elements of the Special Presidential Division (*Division Special Présidentielle*, DSP), the much-feared Military Intelligence Bureau (*Service d'Action et de Renseignement Militaire*, SARM) and the Civil Guard to carry out punitive expeditions – supposedly against rioters, but primarily against political opposition – further alienating allies both at home and abroad. As the unrest spread, the military began experiencing a gradual loss of cohesion. The declining economic situation, grossly neglected infrastructure, endemic corruption, lack of training and poor communication links to the capital and other army units, brought the entire military to the verge of collapse. Without pay for extended periods, most officers began selling fuel and equipment on the black market. When these resources became scarce, they began imposing cuts, or protection rackets, on mining companies, or offering transport services to them.

French and Belgian interventions of 1991

When discipline and unit cohesion broke down, open revolt erupted. On 22 September 1991, the troops of the 31st Airborne Brigade of the Zairian Army mutinied and occupied Kinshasa-N'Djili International Airport. Other units joined them, together with inhabitants of the Zairian capital's southern slums. Looting and destruction spread, aimed mainly at government offices and houses and enterprises belonging to foreigners. The troops of the 41st Commando Brigade stationed in Kisangani followed suit.

Mobutu immediately requested help from Paris and Brussels and, on 23 September, France launched Operation *Baumier*, with the aim of restoring order and evacuating foreign citizens from Kinshasa. With the help of C-160 Transall transports of the ET.61 of the French Air Force (*Armée de l'Air,* AdA), some 450 troops from the 21st Marine Infantry Regiment were deployed from Bangui, in the Central African Republic, to N'Djili IAP – which was meanwhile secured by troops of the SARM under the command of the army's chief of staff, General Donat Lieko Mahele. Another wave of French transports brought in a company of the 2nd Foreign Legion Infantry Regiment from N'Djamena in Chad. The French troops first moved into

Kinshasa to secure the French embassy, before supporting the SARM and the DSP in clearing most of the city centre. Belgian intervention was launched on 24 September, within the frame of Operation *Blue Barn*. Because the Belgians did not consider N'Djili safe enough, they reached an agreement with the government of Brazzaville to land their troops there and then ferry them over the Congo River to Kinshasa. The 450 paras of the *Régiment Para-Comando* arrived from Zaventem in Congo-Brazzaville on board chartered airliners of the national carrier Sabena. Their vehicles and other heavy equipment followed in several Lockheed C-130 Hercules transports of the 205 Squadron/15th Transport Wing of the Belgian Air Force. More heavy equipment and additional troops followed on board Lockheed C-141 StarLifter transports of the United States Air Force (USAF). With a logistics base firmly in place, the Belgians then launched Operation *Kir*, within which they deployed additional paratroopers directly to N'Dolo, the smaller airfield in Kinshasa. By 27 September, they had deployed an additional 850 paratroopers to Zaire.

Meanwhile, the French followed this pattern and temporarily deployed two C-130s and two SA 330 Puma helicopters in Brazzaville. By 27 September, they had secured the airports in Kolwezi and Kisangani, in the face of light and sporadic resistance, before the Belgians deployed around 250 troops to secure Lubumbashi.

With this, the Belgians had around 1,100 and the French around 1,000 troops in the country. They secured all the major airports, enabling them to launch the evacuation of foreign citizens. For this purpose, the Belgian Air Force deployed half a dozen C-130s, while the French used at least ten C-160s, two C-130s and a single Douglas DC-8. This sizeable force was augmented by four C-130s of the Portuguese Air Force. Belgian and French operations were successfully concluded in October 1991 by when over 2,000 expatriates had been evacuated.

All foreign troops had left Zaire by February 1992 when Mobutu deployed the DPS to brutally suppress peaceful protests of hundreds of thousands of Kinois demanding the reopening of the National Conference. As an ever-increasing number of dissidents returned

DSP troops in typical uniform, armed with Israeli Galil assault rifles. *Photo Albert Grandolini Collection*

(primarily to eastern Zaire), they found themselves exposed to brutal oppression and, after a series of ethnically motivated pogroms in 1992/93, some of the opposition parties began accumulating arms. Negotiations between these parties and the government failed and, by 1992, some of them began attacking government authorities and the military along the borders with Angola and Rwanda. During their earlier operations these insurgents had captured considerable amounts of arms and ammunition and their subsequent attacks resulted in a new cycle of violence, culminating on 22 December 1992, when the soldiers of the 41st Brigade in Kisangani again revolted. Without foreign support, Mobutu again ordered a deployment of elements of the DPS. However, the Guards not only became involved in the undue violence and torture of arrested civilians, but also in acts of punitive rampage, which encouraged more people to join the insurgents. The government never proved ready or even interested in finding a finite solution acceptable to all the parties involved.

Children of 59ers

Instability in Zaire caused by the declining economic situation is only a single facet to the background of the subsequent war. A far more murderous reason was provided by differences between various ethnic groups. Indeed, after ultimately abolishing the promised reforms, Mobutu and his aides began concentrating on fomenting inter-ethnic violence. The biggest ethnic conflict in Zaire was that between the Hutus and the Tutsis – both originating from the area today known as Rwanda and Burundi – but who, as mentioned, over time, had spilled into several neighbouring countries.

Uganda had gained independence from Great Britain in October 1962, and was then ravaged by a series of civil wars. These began spilling over into the Congo in 1979 after the government of dictator Idi Amin was toppled in the course of a war with Tanzania. Following this conflict, a number of political parties emerged, including the Uganda Patriotic Movement (UPM) led by a former intelligence officer of the Ugandan military, Yoweri Kaguta Museveni – a MunyaNkole from the Rwanda border area with family connections to the Rwandan exile community in Uganda. During the course of another civil war, between 1981 and 1986, the UPM was reorganized to create the National Resistance Army (NRA). The NRA consisted of several thousand youths, cultivated, indoctrinated, armed and trained by Museveni, excelling through its disciplined and professional combat tactics. As such, it was a striking contrast to the official Ugandan army, which not only exhibited all the signs of lack of discipline, but also had a notorious record for the atrocious and brutal treatment of the population. Between 1984 and 1985, the NRA established control over large swaths of territory and, following the government's lack of readiness to negotiate, the NRA attacked Kampala, the Ugandan capital in January 1986, toppling the government of Tito Okello. Museveni became the president of Uganda. The NRA was subsequently considerably enlarged and reorganized as the national army and renamed the Uganda People's Defence Forces (UPDF) in 1995.

In early 1986, around 500 of some 6,000 NRA fighters were ethnic Banyarawandas, predominantly Tutsi refugees from Rwanda. They contributed significantly to Museveni's victory. One of them, General Fred Rwigyema, was second-in-command of the NRA. It was later established that the reason for this NRA composition was that Museveni shared the Tutsi worldview – the ultimate formation of a

Yoweri Museveni, president of Uganda. *Photo US DoD*

confederation centred in Africa's central Rift Valley under hegemonic control of Tutsi rulers in Uganda, Rwanda and Burundi – and using it to achieve power.

The reason for the presence of Rwandan refugees in Uganda was a series of ethnic conflicts and civil wars that date back to the 19th century. According to popular Tutsi mythology, the highlands of what are today Rwanda and Burundi were feudal kingdoms where the Tutsi aristocracy ruled over masses of Hutus. Over time, the Hutus became convinced that the Tutsis intend to enslave them and that they must be resisted at all costs. Indeed, when the Germans arrived in the area in the mid-19th century, they found Tutsi King Rwabugili struggling with a predominantly Hutu population and launching campaigns against the territories that are now part of Uganda, Burundi and the Congo, but never gaining effective control over any of them. Nevertheless, the Germans – who administered the future Rwanda and Burundi as the colony of Rwanda-Urundi from 1897 until 1914, and the Belgians who administered Rwanda-Urundi as a mandate territory from 1914 until independence in 1962 – helped the Tutsi kings assert their authority over the Tutsi minority and the Hutu majority. The Belgian colonial authorities continued empowering the Tutsi aristocracy and cementing the second-class status of the Hutus. The Tutsi monarchy was abolished following a wave of riots and massacres in 1959. This cycle of violence continued through the 1960s with leading Tutsis launching insurgencies and murdering Hutus, and Hutus retaliating with large-scale slaughter and repression of the Tutsis. This forced many of the elite Tutsis to flee to Uganda where they became known as the '59ers'.

In 1973, chief of staff of the *Forces Armées Rwandaises* (Rwandan Army, FAR) Juvénal Habyarimana, a Hutu, took power in a military coup in Kigali. Although continuing the Hutu discrimination of some of his political predecessors, he did reduce the violence and introduce some degree of economic prosperity. Meanwhile, the Banyarawandas in Uganda continued plotting against him. By the mid-1980s, many of their children were highly educated and had established ties with the USA and Britain. Before Museveni came to power, Uganda had some of harshest refugee laws in the region. Refugees were confined to designated camps and refugee status was transferred between generations: children born in Uganda from refugee parents were themselves considered refugees. However, the refugee status gave children access to United Nations aid, and scholarships from the UN High Commissioner for Refugees (UNHCR) in particular. A number of Banyarwandas thus received

Tutsi refugees – mainly orphans – in southern Uganda, February 1964. Many of them were to play a crucial role in the future of several Central Africa countries. *Photo Mark Lepko Collection*

Fred Rwigyema, a Bayarawanda who grew up in Ugandan refugee camps, joined Museveni early and eventually reached the rank of major-general and the position of deputy commander of the NRA. During the mid-1980s he played a crucial role in the establishment of the RPA. *Photo NakedChiefs*

Major Paul Kagame with RPA troops, 1993. *Photo Mark Lepko Collection*

good education and many sided with the NRA very early on, thus obtaining not only significant combat experience but also additional education in Western military schools. Furthermore, Museveni let them establish their own organizations with the aim of their returning to power in Rwanda.

Using the structure of the 59ers' original organization in Uganda, the Rwandese Alliance for National Unity, the Bayarawandas established a new, militant opposition to the government of President Habyarimana in 1987, the Rwandan Patriotic Front (RPF), with its military wing the Rwandan Patriotic Army (RPA). The RPA came into being as a part of the NRA and, when its fighters initiated a war against the government in Kigali, they practically deserted their posts in the Ugandan military. On 1 October 1990, a cadre of about 50 RPA officers launched a swift advance on the Rwandan capital, Kigali. Although reinforced by around 600 followers and nearly reaching their target, the insurgents were stopped by FAR units under the command of Colonel Augustin Bizimungu, supported by Zairian and French troops, and then suffered a major setback when Fred Rwigyema was killed (possibly in the course of an argument with his sub-commanders, but officially by a stray bullet). They were subsequently forced to retreat in disarray into the mountainous border region where the RPA regrouped under Colonel Paul Kagame – a Bayarawanda and the former head of NRA military intelligence – to launch a classic insurgency campaign.

Rwandan Genocide

After two years of bitter fighting, some of which degenerated into trench warfare, the war between the Rwandan government and the RPA reached a stalemate and the two sides entered into peace negotiations that resulted in the Arusha Accords, signed on 12 July 1992, in Tanzania. This agreement fixed a timetable for an end to the fighting and political talks that would lead to power sharing, but the fighting continued and, following another RPA advance in February 1993, Paris felt concerned enough to order the deployment of over 1,000 French troops to Rwanda. In light of this development, and although approaching to only 30km from Kigali, on 20 February 1993, the RPA declared a unilateral ceasefire and re-opened negotiations with the government. While returning from another round of negotiations in Tanzania, President Habyarimana was assassinated,

together with President Cyprien Ntaryamira of Burundi, when the Dassault Falcon 50 jet carrying them (registration 9XR-NN) was shot down by two MANPADs while approaching to land at Kigali International Airport (IAP) on 6 April 1994.[*]

The assassination of Habyarimana set off a violent reaction by the Rwandan Presidential Guard, but foremost the *Interhamwe* (One Together) and other Hutu paramilitaries who enjoyed the backing of top officials within the government and the FAR. They began killing opposition politicians, prominent Tutsis, and even moderate Hutus. The frenzied massacres that followed cannot be properly described. During the first day of mass slaughter over 1,000 people were killed in Kigali alone. Twenty-four hours later, the number of victims had climbed to more than 10,000, with no end in sight. This wholesale murder of the Tutsis and moderate Hutus in Rwanda between April and mid-July 1994 is known as the Rwandan Genocide, a poor description for the mass slaughter of an estimated 800,000–930,000 people – or about 20% of the country's total population.

---

[*] There is still some controversy surrounding the downing of this aircraft and the assassination of the two presidents. While some theories saw the involvement of the leading RPA cadres, the generally accepted version is that it was shot down by Hutu extremists within the Rwandan Presidential Guard opposed to a negotiated peace with the Tutsis, that they saw as 'selling out' of Hutu interests.

Wreckage of the Falcon 50 that was carrying presidents Juvénal Habyarimana and Cyprien Ntaryamira when it was shot down by Hutu extremists on 6 April 1994. *Photo Pit Weinert Collection*

An endless column of Rwandan refugees streaming over the border from Rwanda into Zaire in May1994. The arrival of around 1.2 million Rwandan Hutus and Twa overwhelmed the local Zairian authorities and international aid organizations present in the Kivus. No one could have predicted at the time what these people would endure in the following years, and what kind of repercussions their presence would have on the stability of the entire Central African region in the following two decades. *Photo Mark Lepko Collection*

The assassination of Juvénal Habyarimana, president of Rwanda, seen in this photo from the 1980s, sparked a series of endless tragedies that are still destabilizing much of Central Africa. *Photo US DoD*

The Rwandan Genocide shocked practically everybody inside and outside Rwanda but, initially, very little was done to stop it. Belgium attempted to deploy an intervention force with the intention of extracting own and UN troops hemmed in and around Kigali, but its C-130 transports were prevented from landing at the country's only international airport – in Kigali – because runways were reportedly blocked by RPA troops. Their second attempt, on 9 April, was more successful and Belgians and French troops were eventually able to secure the airport, enabling a number of chartered civilian and military transports to evacuate around 430 surviving expatriates and UN soldiers during the following days. Their efforts were supported by at least one Lockheed C-5A Galaxy, two Lockheed C-141B StarLifters and four C-130s of the USAF that flew additional evacuees out to Nairobi in Kenya.

Pre-occupied with a host of emergencies around the world, including Bosnia, Haiti, Iraq and North Korea, the UN response remained slow during the following weeks. Furthermore, the recent US withdrawal from Somalia supposedly forced the hand of US representatives to the UN to veto a resolution calling for the deployment of a 5,000-strong contingent of peacekeepers to Rwanda, on 17 May. Following additional negotiations on 18 June, Paris announced its intention to deploy troops to the country and establish a safe zone in southwestern Rwanda. Sanctioned by the UN, Operation *Turquoise* was launched on 23 June and the first of what would become 2,550 French troops and 500 troops from Chad, Guinea-Bissau, Egypt, Mauritania, Niger and Senegal arrived in Kigali. Tasked with stopping the mass killings and protecting the integrity and population of Rwanda, this turned into a much-belated effort that primarily resulted in interposing French military forces between the advancing RPA and the parts of Rwanda still under the nominal control of the remnants of the FAR, as well as the Interhamwe militia.

After issuing a warning that it would restart the war if the killing did not stop, the RPA launched a new offensive. In spite of some resistance by the French, the insurgents defeated the FAR and seized control of most of the country, including Kigali, which was secured on 3/4 July. The official army then practically disintegrated, falling back toward the towns of Ruhengeri and Gisenyi, before capitulating on 18 July 1994. In a decision that was foremost symbolic by nature, the RPF subsequently appointed Pasteur Bizimungu, a Hutu who had joined it in 1990, as the new president, while Kagame was appointed vice-president and minister of defence. For all practical purposes, Kagame was the actual strongman, pulling the strings from behind the scenes.

The defeat of the FAR resulted in an exodus of hundreds of thousands of Hutus to Zaire, and nominally to Burundi, Tanzania and Uganda, as the RPA became involved in atrocities, not only against the Hutu, but also against the minority Twa population which suffered a massive loss of life while survivors were forced to flee. As

The Kigali memorial for victims of the 1994 Rwandan Genocide.
Photo Creative Commons

A USAF C-141 StarLifter at Nairobi IAP in Kenya after evacuating expatriates from Rwanda and Burundi on 10 April 1994.
Photo US DoD

French paratroopers evacuate foreigners from Kigali, April 1994.
Photo Pellizzari Xavier/Savriacouty Claude, ECPA-ECPAD

the RPF established itself in power in Rwanda, between July and August 1994, an estimated 1.2 million refugees gathered in dozens of camps in eastern Zaire alone, over 200,000 in Burundi, while more than 2 million people were still on the run inside Rwanda.

On 22 July 1994, US President Clinton launched *Operation Support Hope*, ordering a contingent of around 2,100 troops and multiple heavy transports to provide immediate relief to the refugees. Two days later, transport aircraft of the USAF began landing at Kigali, Goma (in Zaire), Entebbe (Uganda) and Mombasa (Kenya). Operation *Support Hope* reached its peak in August that year when around 2,350 US service members were deployed to Rwanda and its neighbouring countries. Except for delivering around 15,000 tons of humanitarian aid, US transport aircraft were also used to transport Ethiopian and other UN peacekeeping contingents for deployment in Rwanda.

However, the war and mass murder in Rwanda did not stop in July 1994. Although the French forces of Operation *Turquoise* handed over the area they controlled on 21 August 1994, the new government in Kigali continued pursuing and herding the refugees, accusing the UN of "feeding the killers" and forcing most foreign aid organizations to leave. Only the UN contingent was left in the country by April 1995, when the RPA troops advanced into the remaining refugee camps along the border with Burundi and began evictions at gunpoint. Lacking authorization and the necessary firepower, the UN peacekeepers could only watch helplessly. At one point the RPA herded 80,000 men, women and children onto a long, narrow ridge over Kibeho, supposedly for 'processing'. Without water, food, medicine or latrines their plight was pitiful. Hutu extremists then began goading the civilians into protest, and lining up behind them they cut down dozens with machetes, forcing the survivors to try and break through the RPA lines. As the refugees fled down the hill, the Tutsi soldiers manning the outer cordon opened fire. Thousands were shot, even though the desperate mass eventually broke through the barriers, leaving behind between 2,000 and 5,000 bodies. Most of the Hutu extremists managed to escape across the border into Burundi and then into eastern Zaire.

Ethnic conflicts and the refugee crisis

At the time Rwandan refugees began flowing over the border into eastern Zaire in April 1994, the government in Kinshasa was already at odds with two Rwandan ethnic groups: the Banyamasassi and the Banyamulenge. During the 1920s, the Belgian colonial authorities began importing labour, primarily Tutsis but also some Hutus, from Rwanda to the Kivu Province. Over time these people constituted powerful and wealthy communities in North Kivu (where they were called Banyamasassi) and South Kivu (where they were called Banyamulenge); some even established themselves as successful businessmen in Kinshasa. Upon independence, they were granted Congolese nationality but during the civil wars of 1960–65 they found themselves in conflict with various local tribes. This they concluded successfully after siding with the emerging Mobutu, but native Congolese continued disputing their nationality, an issue which was never resolved. Under pressure from several sides, in 1991, Mobutu decided to simply drop the Banyamulenge. He issued a law on citizenship and overnight declared that the Banyamulenge were no longer entitled to Congolese citizenship and would forego all Congolese rights. As the unrest and instability spread in March 1993, several ethnic groups attacked Banyamulenge in North Kivu,

One of ten SA.330B Puma helicopters of the French Army Aviation (*Armée de l'Air de Terre*, ALAT) deployed in Rwanda in the course of Operation Turquoise, between June and September 1994. *Photo Pellizzari Xavier/Savriacouty Claude, ECPA-ECPAD*

Once the international community realized that it had failed to prevent the genocide of Tutsis and moderate Hutus in Rwanda, it scrambled to help survivors. Here a Lockheed C-141 StarLifter of the 452nd Air Wing US Air Force unloads relief aid for Rwandan refugees in Goma, eastern Zaire, late 1994. *Photo US DoD*

Paul Kagame with RPA fighters shortly after the successful conclusion of the civil war in which he led the RPA to victory. *Photo NakedChiefs*

Through the rest of 1994 and into 1995, Western powers continued sending relief aid to Rwanda, apparently paying little attention to an entirely new set of tensions and the military build-up around them, which were soon to spill over into neighbouring Zaire. Here a column of US Army trucks, loaded with water for refugees, is underway in Rwanda, late 1994. *Photo US DoD*

killing as many as 7,000 and forcing an estimated 300,000 to flee. In South Kivu local officials, backed by the newly established transitional parliament in Kinshasa, launched a campaign of intimidation against the Banyamulenge. Once again, the DSP was deployed to quell the unrest. The Guards, by now unpaid for an extended period, first joined the looters, then began pursuing them with extreme brutality. Hundreds of soldiers were arrested and summarily executed.

The arrival of the huge numbers of Hutu refugees in eastern Zaire resulted in an extreme humanitarian crisis that developed inside the emerging refugee camps situated primarily in the Bukavu area, in mid-1994. Thousands died of malnutrition and from epidemics. Allegiances were not the same in all the camps; the majority were of a purely civilian nature and many of the inhabitants subsequently grouped under the aegis of such moderate organizations as the Republican Rally for Democracy in Rwanda (*Rassemblement Démocratique pour le Rwanda*, RDR), but others were exclusively occupied by members of former Rwandan establishment, ex-FAR officers and other ranks and their families, involved in the Rwandan Genocide.

Fiercely anti-Tutsi and leaning toward supporting the Rwandan Hutus, on 28 April 1995 the National Conference in Kinshasa adopted a series of resolutions targeting primarily the Banyamulenge, treating them as refugees, accusing them of fraudulently securing Zairian citizenship and calling for their expulsion. Actually, the government exercised only weak control over the east of the country, primarily the

provinces of North and South Kivu, where the Hutu refugees had settled. Indeed, the locally based FAZ units and police were hopelessly outnumbered by the Hutu militants alone, and thus were not in a position to follow the order and expel the Banyamulenge. Furthermore, local Zairian officials and military commanders found that dealing with desperate refugees and former Rwandan officials and ex-FAR seeking not only safety, but also arms and ammunition, was a lucrative business, and most of them soon become involved with the Hutus, the UN and various NGOs active in the area, rather than following orders from Kinshasa. In early 1996, ethnic violence also spread through eastern Zaire because the indigenous Nyangas and Hundes, as well as different Mayi-Mayi militias, continued assaulting the Banyamulenge, murdering hundreds. This was something the newly established RPA government in Kigali found entirely unacceptable. After its repeated warnings of the activity of the extremist Hutus and violence against the Banyamulenge remained ignored by the West, the Tutsi leadership of Rwanda decided it was time to act.

Thus, because of stirring trouble with the Banyamulenge, collaborating with Hutu extremists and his earlier interventions in neighbouring countries, Mobutu found himself on a collision course with the RPF in Rwanda.

CHAPTER TWO:
OPPOSING FORCES

The First Congo War (also known as the War of National Liberation), fought in 1996 and 1997, involved a wide range of very different armed groups, including the regular armed forces of Zaire, supported by UNITA insurgents from Angola, fighting against regular Rwandan and Ugandan militaries, supported by various Zairian insurgent organizations, and – later on – the regular Angolan military.

Zairian armed forces
The history of the Congolese armed forces dates back to 4 August 1888 when Belgium's King Léopold II, governor of the independent state of the Congo, established the *Force Publique*, a private militia composed of foreign mercenaries and Congolese, trained by Belgian officers, and responsible for the protection of economic exploitation. The force was significantly expanded and deployed in combat during the First and Second World Wars when it became involved in a number of campaigns in East Africa. On independence in 1960, the *Force Publique* was still run by Belgian officers. This caused a mutiny and a rapid Africanization of its officer corps which led to further problems because, after the expulsion of the Belgians, the military faced a lack of skills at practically every level. To remedy the situation NCOs above the rank of sergeant were commissioned to the officer ranks. Many of these instantly began meddling in politics, resulting in a civil war. Although an officer training school was established in Luluabourg (now Kananga) in early 1961, providing relatively good services to the ANC, the Congolese National Army, once Mobutu had established himself in power he invited six nations to assist in rebuilding the military as an effective fighting force. Belgium trained the ground forces, Italy the air force, Norway the naval element, Israel the paratroopers and commandos, and Canada the communications and transport units. With the help of foreign advisers, additional high-level training centres were established during the 1970s. These proved so successful that students from other countries – including Burundi, Central African Republic, Chad, Niger, Rwanda and Togo – were also trained there. Considering internal security to be the main threat, foreign advisers moulded the army – renamed the Zairian Armed Forces (*Forces Armées Zairoise*, FAZ) in 1971 – in COIN warfare, primarily against various dissident and separatist movements. The FAZ was based on a large element of light infantry supported by paratroopers and commandos. Armour and mechanized and artillery units remained relatively small. Climatic circumstances, rugged terrain, dense jungle, lack of roads and a lack of support infrastructure and know-how all but made the operation of large mechanized forces impossible. The army was thus equipped with very little armour – mainly French-made AML-60 and AML-90 armoured cars and a small brigade equipped with Chinese-made light and main battle tanks (MBTs), and a few artillery pieces. Instead, for the purpose of protecting borders and national parks the Civil Guard was established in 1984, although this was subsequently incorporated into the army.

Starting in 1975, Mobutu began focusing the FAZ's task primarily on domestic law enforcement. Thus the army became critical in enabling the government to exercise control throughout the country. Furthermore, he began creating privileged units, mainly consisting of his tribal allies, and then transforming the military into a specialized organ for his own political party, the Popular Revolution Movement (*Mouvement Populaire de la Revolution*, MPR), in turn resulting in the politicization and tribalization, as well as the de-professionalization, that ultimately destroyed the FAZ.

Except for exercising political power as president of the Republic of Zaire, Mobutu also acted as the minister of defence, president of the Superior Council of Defence, supreme commander and commander-in-chief, thus subjecting the military to his sole authority. He personally promoted and dismissed officers, ordered matériel and directed military operations. Further down the chain of command were three regional headquarters – the first in Lubumbashi, the second in Kisangani and the third in Kinshasa – the commanders of which were subordinated to the local civilian authorities and political officers, carefully selected for their loyalty from the ranks of the MPR. With the help of such commando structures and by taking care not to let any military officers hold cabinet positions, and by regularly shuffling senior military posts, the government asserted that no officers could develop an independent support base within the FAZ. Under such circumstances, the influence of the acting chief of staff, General Donat Lieko Mahele – graduate of the prestigious French military academy at Saint-Cyr, who established himself as Mobutu's best field commander by recapturing the port of Moba from Kabila's PRP in 1984 – was very limited.

Nominal strength of the FAZ in the mid-1970s climbed to over 80,000 officers and other ranks, but through the early 1990s declined to around 45,000. The force was maintained by voluntary enlistment. Women were permitted to join not only the army but even special corps like the paratroopers. (Major FAZ units as at 1990 are shown in Table 1 on page 16.)

From the standpoint of the government, the most important elements of the FAZ were Mobutu's personal guards, known as *le Hiboux* (the Owls), who were all members of the Ngandi tribe and had been trained abroad. This training was roughly comparable to the average US or Western European SWAT outfits in terms of armament and capabilities. The major military intelligence agency was the National Service for Intelligence and Protection (*Service National d'Intelligence et Protection*, SNIP), led by General Likulia Bolongo. The most important unit of the army was the Special Presidential Division (*Division Présidentielle Speciale*, DPS). This nominally 15,000-strong force, organized into two commando brigades and the Dragon Battalion, was under the command of Mobutu's nephew, General Nzimbi Ngbale, and was responsible for the defence and security of Kinshasa. The DPS troops were reasonably trained, by some 40 Israeli contract personnel, among others, provided by the Lavdan Company on contract to Kinshasa in 1994. Most of the DPS's recruits were from the Ngbaka tribe but it was led by officers from the Nbgandi, the president's tribe. Members of *le Hiboux* and the DPS were always paid regularly, were well fed and enjoyed numerous

An AML-90 armoured reconnaissance scout car and an AML-60 (back) of the FAZ, in the early 1980s. During this period the FAZ purchased a total of 95 AML-60s and 60 AML-90s. *Photo Albert Grandolini Collection*

privileges by comparison with the rest of the military. Something similar can be said of the Civil Guard (*Garde Civile*), which was a political militia of sorts, consisting entirely of Ngandi tribe members under the command of General Baramoto Kpama Kata, another relative of Mobutu, and which was some 10,000 strong. Furthermore, the SARM maintained its own armed wing, some 1,000-strong mostly Nbgandi, under General Bolozi Gbudu Tanikpa, Mobutu's brother-in-law. However, all these units obeyed only the president and not FAZ staff, and neither Nzimbi nor Baramoto were professional soldiers but rather politicians/businessmen.

The Israeli-trained 41st Commando Brigade based in Kisangani was the most important intervention force in the northeastern part of the country. Similarly, based in Kamina, in the west of the country, the French-trained 31st Airborne Brigade was considered crucial to the defence of its borders with Congo-Brazzaville and Angola.

Cooperating with the army was the small navy, which included the Coast, River and Lake Guards. Nominally around 1,500 strong (including a battalion of 600 marines) and with its main base in Banana, near Matadi, in western Congo, this force was equipped with a miscellany of Chinese-built Shanghai II fast-attack craft and Huchuan class patrol vessels, plus around 24 Arcoa and Swift Mk II coastal class patrol craft, many of which were not operational by 1990.

Force Aérienne Zaïroise

Considering the local terrain and poor land communications and the existence of 100 airfields and airstrips and four major air bases left by the Belgians, it is unsurprising that air power played an important role in the capabilities of the Zairian military, and that it experienced

a phase of significant development during the 1960s and 1970s. Already established on independence as *Aviation de la Force République du Congo*, the Zairian Air Force (*Force Aérienne Zaïroise*, FAZA), as it was in the early 1990s, came into being during the late 1960s. A few native pilots and ground personnel were trained by Belgian instructors, and one former Luftwaffe colonel, on a small number of North American T-6G Texans in the early 1960s, before Italy was contracted to take over the role as major supervisor of the fledgling air force. The Italians established a pilot training school at N'Dolo airfield in 1962, equipped with ten T-6s provided from surplus stocks of their air force, but this was closed followed by a series of fatal and near-fatal accidents, including one in which the leader of the Italian team was severely injured. Overall, by early 1963, only eleven Congolese pilots, 38 technicians and two aerial-photo interpreters completed their training with Italian help. None of them was considered combat-capable and thus saw no action during the civil war that was to rage until 1967. Nevertheless, the Italians remained influential and launched a new effort, advising the government in Kinshasa to purchase 15 Piaggio P148 basic trainers, which proved more suitable for initial pilot training. A training squadron equipped with this type was established in October 1964, by which time the balance of the air force consisted of the US-run Anstalt Wigmo contingent manned by exiled Cuban pilots, who flew a miscellany of North American T-28 Trojans, Douglas B-26K Invaders, Curtiss C-46 Commandos and Beechcraft C-45 transports, as well as Bell 47 and Vertol-Piasecki H-21 helicopters. The following year, a group of Congolese pilots was sent to Marignane in France to be trained on Aérospatiale SE 316B Alouette III helicopters, 15 of which were

Table 1: *Forces Armées Zaïroise*, 1990

Unit	Area of Responsibility	Notes
Special Presidential Division	Kinshasa	Consisting of two commando brigades and the Dragon Battalion; CO General Nzimbi
Kamanyola (Infantry) Division	Shaba Province	Including the 11th, 12th, and 14th infantry brigades, each with two infantry battalions and one support battalion; only 14th Brigade was combat ready
1st (Independent) Armoured Brigade	Mbanza-Ngungu	Only 30 operational tanks
13th (Independent) Infantry Brigade	Kalemie	Consisting of three infantry battalions and one support battalion; one of the most neglected FAZ units
21st (Independent) Infantry Brigade (Leopard Infantry)	Lubumbashi	Consisting of two infantry battalions and one support battalion with modest combat capability
22nd (Independent) Light Infantry Brigade	Kamina	Consisting of two infantry battalions and one support battalion with modest combat capability
31st Parachute Brigade	Kinshasa	Consisting of 311th and 312th para battalions and one support battalion; high state of combat readiness
32nd Parachute Brigade	Kitona	Established in 1987/88 and still in the process of build-up
41st Commando Brigade	Kisangani	Consisting of 411th, 412th, and 413th commando battalions and one support battalion

Female paratroopers of the Israeli-trained 12th Airborne Battalion (later 312th Para Battalion) FAZ. *Photo Gianni Meocci*

The small Zairian naval arm was never properly maintained and most of its ships were inoperable by 1990. This photograph shows two Shanghai II class fast-attack craft (hull numbers 104 and 105), equipped with four 37mm and four 25mm guns. *Photo Mark Lepko Collection*

purchased, as well as 12 T-6s, also from France. At least four of these aircraft were lost in fighting against mercenaries in May 1967 when six of the Congolese pilots flew their first combat sorties on T-28s.

Meanwhile, in November 1966, the air force was reorganized into two groups, each of which had three wings, in turn consisting of three squadrons. The No. 1 Group included the 11th Transport Wing, predominantly manned by foreigners flying transport aircraft, and the 12th Tactical Support Wing, equipped with T-6s and Alouettes and manned by Congolese and Belgian crews. The Italian-run training squadron was expanded to become the 13th Wing, consisting of one preparatory pilot training squadron (responsible for recruitment and selection), one elementary pilot training squadron, and one advanced training squadron. However, the No. 2 Group still consisted exclusively of Anstalt Wingmo crews and their US-supplied aeroplanes and helicopters, most of which were withdrawn from the Congo by 1968 and redeployed to South East Asia. In order to re-equip No. 2 Group in April that year, the Congolese and Italians signed a new treaty regarding technical assistance and, in May 1968, the air force launched a recruitment campaign, intending to find and train enough new pilots to replace the foreigners. Simultaneously, a decision was taken to purchase 17 Aermacchi MB 326 jet trainers (nicknamed 'Sukisa' by the Congolese) and 12 SIAI-Marchetti SF 260MC piston-engined trainers. Corresponding contracts were signed soon thereafter.

Despite continuous Italian supervision, and the presence of a technical team from Aermacchi, the efforts to train Congolese pilots and ground crews saw limited success. Through the late 1960s and early 1970s, the 13th Wing received an average intake of around 40 Congolese students a year, but less than half of these completed their training, partially because of various problems with students and numerous fatal accidents, but also because the foreigners were not particularly interested in losing their lucrative jobs. Out of 720 candidates applying to become pilots in 1971, only 20 were accepted, with 13 sent to Italy for advanced training. The other seven attended courses in France, where they trained to fly Alouette IIIs and the 12 newly ordered Aérospatiale SA 330C Pumas, which began arriving in June 1971. Only three Congolese pilots were trained on MB 326s (at Aermacchi's facility in Lecce, Italy), before the first three MB 326s reached N'Djili on 24 November 1969. Although the number of pilots gradually increased through the mid-1970s, and in spite of supposedly positive experiences, the FAZA never became completely self-sufficient in operations and maintenance of this type – even after all 17 aircraft were delivered and entered service with one training asset and two operational squadrons (one based at N'Djili and the other at Kamina). Furthermore, most of the pilots selected to fly

A handful of ex-Belgian T-6G Texan trainers formed the basis of original military aviation of the Congo in the early 1960s. They were flown by a group of Belgian pilots who trained the Congolese within the 21st Squadron. *Photo Vandenbon*

Zairian MB 326 pilots prepare for a sortie from N'Djili, early 1970s. *Photo Gianni Meocci*

Top view of a Zairian MB 326 *Sukisa*. Notable are large roundels applied on the top and bottom surfaces of both wings. The type was nicknamed 'Sukisa' in service with the FAZA.
Photo Jean-Pierre Sonck Collection

One of three DHC-5D Buffalos purchased by Zaire in the early 1970s. Only two of these aircraft remained intact by 1996 and only one of them was still operational. *Photo Albert Grandolini Collection*

Sukisas were promoted to their positions due to political and tribal connections rather than flying skills.*

Despite such problems, and significant financial difficulties, in 1970 Mobutu ordered seven Lockheed C-130 Hercules transports from the USA and three DHC-5D Buffalo transports from Canada. The fleet of light transports, liaison and training aircraft was further reinforced through the acquisition of 16 Reims-Cessna FRA 150Ms and FTB 337Gs (which could be armed and used as light fighter-bombers). The helicopter fleet was reinforced with five additional Alouette IIIs.

Finally, in 1972, Zaire entered negotiations with France for the acquisition of 17 Dassault Mirage 5 fighter-bombers, including 14 single-seaters and three twin-seater conversion trainers. The conversion of FAZA pilots and technicians to this type was undertaken in Dijon, France, and was completed in Zaire by Belgian and French instructors. Based at Kamina, the Mirages entered service with the newly established 21st Wing, but not all were delivered as a result of financial problems caused by the declining copper price. Zaire was eventually able to pay for only eight Mirage 5Ms and three Mirage 5DMs. Furthermore, two single-seaters (including the serialled M401) had been written off in accidents by 1978 and one

(M402) during its deployment in Chad in 1983. The last three intact Mirages – including twin-seaters M201 and M203 – were resold to France, where they were last seen in 1996.

The acquisition of six additional MB 326Ks (dedicated strike variant, with only one cockpit) in 1983, temporarily improved the situation of units equipped with the type. Three of these were deployed in Chad that year and participated in the parade on the 20th anniversary of Mobutu's rise to power in July 1986. However, by the early 1990s, all eight surviving MB 326GB/Ks and around 20 SF 260MCs had to be stored for lack of maintenance. Worse yet, by 1995, the FAZA ceased keeping even their remaining C-130s in operational condition, although two, coded 9T-TCC and 9T-TCF, were sent to France for overhaul in 1996; they never returned and were subsequently taken up by the French Air Force (*Armee de l'Air*, AdA). A pair of Buffalos, one SA 330 Puma and a handful of Alouette IIIs were all that remained on active service with the FAZA, and even these were mainly used for VIP transport or smuggling purposes.

The air force also never resolved its problem of the shortage of pilots. Although around 2,500 strong for most of the 1980s, less than 20 FAZA pilots ever became fully qualified to fly MB 326s and Mirages – and the best Congolese Mirage pilot, Colonel Leon Mbo, was killed in a catastrophic loss of a C-130H that exploded after taking off from N'Djili, under suspicious circumstances, on 20 April 1990.

Therefore, although theoretically still an imposing force, the FAZA was all but non-operational by 1990, and its last known order of

---

* For reports of the FAZA becoming 'virtually self-sufficient' in operating MB 326s, see *Congolese Air Force Operating MB 326GBs,* AW&ST, 1971; for comparison, see works by Jean-Pierre Sonck cited in the bibliography.

battle, as illustrated in Table 2 on page 19, is of rather limited meaning – except as an indication for what types of stored aircraft could be found at which air bases.

Combat experiences of the FAZ

Over time, the FAZ and the FAZA saw combat deployments in a number of conflicts, inside and outside the Congo. In 1970, the FAZ units helped the Nigerian Army end the Biafran secession and, in 1971, were deployed in Burundi, where they helped restore the government. However, the deployment of two FAZ battalions in Angola, in support of the US-backed National Front for the Liberation of Angola (FNLA), resulted in a fiasco, during the course of which two battalions of paratroopers disintegrated in the face of enemy resistance, in November 1975. Only half the deployed troops were ever accounted for again, while the rest – excluding casualties – deserted and never reported back to their units.

In retaliation for the ill-fated FAZ intervention, the government in Luanda supported two attempts by ex-Katangan Tigers of the FNLC to invade Zaire. The first attempt began on 8 March 1977, when around 1,500 insurgents crossed the border into Katanga Province (named Shaba between 1971 and 1996) and soon took Mutshatsha, Kisengi, Kasaji, Sandoa and Kapanga.

President Mobutu declared a state of emergency and appealed for help. In Operation *Verveine*, supported by US financial and military aid, the French Air Force deployed 13 C-160 Transall transports to move 1,500 Moroccan troops to Kolwezi and Lubumbashi, starting on 10 April. The FNLC positions in Dilolo, Kasagi, Sandao and Kisenge were repeatedly attacked by FAZA Mirage 5Ms from Kamina- and Kolwezi-based MB 326GBs. Mutshatsha had been retaken by FAZ

and Moroccan troops by late April and the rest of the insurgents were forced to withdraw across the border to Angola by 26 May 1977.

Slightly over a year later, on 11 May 1978, 2,000–2,500 FNLC infiltrated Zaire from Angola and occupied Mutshatsha again. By 13 May, they had overrun the FAZ units protecting Kolwezi and the local airfield, captured over 2,000 European hostages and destroyed two MB 326GBs (serials FG-468 and FG-471; three other aircraft of this type were damaged), six Cessna 310s and several SA 316B and SA 330 helicopters. On 16 May, the FAZ reacted by dropping the 311th Parachute Battalion on Kolwezi from C-130Hs of the 19th Wing, but this operation only resulted in partial success. Retaking the local airfield, the paratroopers were practically annihilated, suffering 60 per cent casualties, and were in no condition to continue fighting. This prompted a combined French–Belgian intervention (the French part of which was codenamed Operation *Leopard* and the Belgian *Red Bean*), in the course of which the 2nd Parachute Regiment of the Foreign Legion was airdropped on Kolwezi on 19 May 1978. The paras cleared the town in two days, despite several counterattacks, and then prepared for a ground advance with the help of vehicles flown in by French and Zairian transports. After committing atrocities against their European and African hostages, and having suffered several hundred dead and captured, the insurgents avoided further direct confrontation and re-crossed the border between 23 and 25 May. The French and Belgian contingents were eventually replaced by a 5,000-strong force of African troops from different countries, brought in on USAF C-141A StarLifters to help the FAZ maintain peace.

These two operations, which became known as Shaba I and Shaba II, revealed inherent weaknesses of the Zairian army. Except for a

The first single-seat Mirage 5M (serial M401) destined for Zaire, photographed while still in France. *Photo Albert Grandolini Collection*

FAZA Colonel Leon Mbo, leading Zairian Mirage pilot, seen while serving as a major during combat operations in the Shaba Province (Katanga) in the late 1970s. *Photo Emmanuel Kandolo Collection*

One of six MB 326Ks delivered to Zaire in 1983. Three of these single-seater light strikers were deployed to support the FAZ contingent in Chad during the same year, but subsequently saw very little service and were eventually stored at N'Djili. *Photo Tom Cooper Collection*

This SA 321J Super Frelon helicopter of the FAZA (registered as 9T-SPF) was equipped for VIP transport.
Photo Albert Grandolini Collection

Table 2: *Force Aérienne Zaïroise*, 1990			
Unit	**Base**	**Type**	**Notes**
1 Groupement Aérien (HQ Kinshasa)			
12e Escadre de Liaison			(12e EdL)
122e Escadrille	N'Dolo	SA 316B, SA 321J, SA 330C, SA 332	Only 3–4 SA 316Bs and 1 SA 330C still operational
13e Escadre d'Entrainement			(13e EdE)
131ere Escadrille d'Ecolage Elementaire	N'Dolo	FRA 150, SF 260MC	Except for 2–3, all aircraft stored
132e Escadrille d'Ecolage Avancé	N'Djili	MB 326GB	All aircraft stored
19e Escadre d'Appui Logistique			(19e EdAL)
191ere Escadrille	N'Djili	C-130H	All aircraft stored
2 Groupement Aérien (HQ Kamina)			
21er Escadre de chasse et d'Assault			(21er EdCA)
211ere Escadrille	Kamina	Mirage 5M, Mirage 5DM	Non-operational; aircraft re-sold to France
212e Escadrille	Kamina	MB 326GB, MB 326K	On detachment from 132e EdEA; non-operational and stored
22e Escadre de Transport Tactique			(22e EdTT)
221ere Escadrille	Kamina	DHC-5D, Cessna 310R	stored

crack paratroop battalion, most FAZ units tended to flee when under fire. Similarly, while crews of transport and helicopter units did their utmost to provide support, the Mirage squadron managed only a few sorties, most of which missed their targets. The situation reached a point where Egypt offered its pilots to reinforce the shaken unit. Congolese MB 326 pilots flew over 300 combat sorties during the course of Shaba I and II, but proved reluctant to engage the enemy because of rumours that the FNLC was armed with SAM-7s. They not only repeatedly missed their targets, but also hit several villages in Angola and Zambia. Some were court martialled as a result.

The FAZ also did little to quell the PRP uprising in northern Shaba, between Kalemie and Moba, of the mid-1980s. Instead, many of its officers entered agreements with Kabila and ameliorated their pay by selling arms to the insurgents. The situation changed once the officers in question increased their demands, prompting the PRP to assault and capture the port of Moba on 13 November 1983. The FAZ mobilized and deployed two battalions, the 311th and the 312th, of the 31st Parachute Brigade, as well as the marines of the 13th (Naval) Infantry Brigade, to drive the PRP from the area; however, nearly all reports about this operation – codenamed Moba I – indicate that it was actually inconclusive. The PRP survived this period intact and most of the insurgents supposedly killed in the course of the fighting for Moba were actually local people upon whom government forces took reprisals for their alleged support of the PRP. This was confirmed by a series of small-scale COIN operations undertaken by FAZ troops during the following years (Moba II), most of which were inconclusive as well. Indeed, although the insurgents who crossed Lake Tanganyika and attacked Moba again on 16 June 1985 were easily repulsed, subsequent operations proved very costly in terms of logistical demands, while producing next to no results. Ultimately, when the FAZA was left without operational Hercules transports and Mirage fighter-bombers, the troops of the 31st Brigade were returned to Kinshasa, leaving a much weakened 13th Infantry Brigade in Kalemie, without any support or equipment necessary to conduct COIN operations. Instead, Mobutu was forced to deploy the better part of the SARM to finish the PRP, before that organization became defunct due to internal splits in 1986/87.

The final foreign deployments of the FAZ and the FAZA experienced success mainly due to French and US logistic support and leadership. In 1982/83, three battalions of the FAZ – supported by small contingents of three each of FAZA's *Sukisas* and *Mirages* – was deployed to Chad in support of President Goukouni Oueddei, who was threatened by a Libyan invasion. Operating with French and US help, this force secured the capital of N'Djamena and the second-most important town, Abéché, without major fighting.

French assistance and leadership secured a successful deployment of the paratroopers of the 31st Brigade in Rwanda in October 1990, in reaction to an RPA offensive against Kigali that saw some bitter battles. Overall, the FAZ proved a loyal, but ineffective force, dependent on foreign advisers, leadership and infusions of money to remain functional.

Rwandan Defence Force

The original Rwandan army (*Forces Armées Rwandaises*, FAR), came into being as the National Guard, established by the Belgian Colonel Guy Logiest, in the aftermath of the unrest that ended the Nyiginya monarchy in Rwanda in 1961. Although under Rwandan control since 1964, the FAR was run with Belgian and French support until it fell apart in July 1994, when the Hutu-dominated government collapsed after the Rwandan Genocide and in the face of the RPA invasion. The major FAR units had consisted of the Presidential Guard, the Paracommando and Reconnaissance battalions and eight infantry companies, mainly staffed by Hutus and trained by the French.[*] These

---

[*] According to former French soldiers (including at least one member of the famous National Gendarmerie Intervention Group, the GIGN), the French not only trained FAR officers and other ranks, but also members of various of Hutu militias, primarily the Interhamwes. See *French Soldiers Trained Rwandan Militia*, AFP, 22 April 2005.

Moroccan troops waiting to board French C-160 Transall transports for deployment against the FNLC in the Katanga/Shaba Province of Zaire, March 1977. *Photo Albert Grandolini Collection*

formations played a key role during the genocide of 1994, before most of their commanders, NCOs and soldiers fled to eastern Zaire.

Over the period 1994–97, the Rwandan Patriotic Army was reorganized as a new national army of Rwanda. It comprised the High Command Council, the general staff, the army (also designated the Rwanda Land Force), an air wing and specialized units. Contrary to the former FAR, which used French as its official language, the RPA's

Kolwezi airfield after it was raided by the FNLC in May 1978. While the MB 326 on the left is completely destroyed, the aircraft to the right came away with relatively light damage. In the background is a C-130H of the Belgian Air Force used to deploy Belgian paratroopers who helped the FAZ quell this short-lived uprising and evacuate surviving Europeans. *Photo Marc Steegmans*

Another view of the same MB 326 destroyed by the FNLC at Kolwezi. *Photo French Ministry of Defence*

official language is English. Despite a minimal defence budget, but with the help of foreign aid between 1994 and 1996, it was boosted in size from around 15,000 to around 40,000 officers and other ranks, organized in six manoeuvring brigades and support services. The organization and areas of responsibility mirrored the political administrative boundaries. (See Table 3 facing.) Each of these brigades usually had three to five battalions, but additional battalions were often added – or subtracted – depending on combat requirements. While most battalions received numerical designations, quite a few are known only by their names.

The force was maintained by voluntary enlistment, officially starting at the age of 18, but between 1995 and 2002, came the frequent practice of forceful recruitment of younger males. In other cases, local tribal chiefs cooperated closely with the RPF and RPA leadership to recruit thousands of volunteers – predominantly jobless youths – by attracting them with promises of regular pay, and the idea of capturing the Kivu provinces in Zaire and incorporating them into Rwanda.

Although the RPA's official mission statement meets international standards, its actual mission is the defence of the Tutsi section of the Rwandan population, and – with few exceptions – includes very few Hutus (between them, several ex-FAR officers, some of whom were often showcased in an effort to augment its rebranding as the Rwanda Defence Force, RDF, in 2002). In fact, for a country where Hutus and Rwandans of mixed descent represent a vast majority of the population – not only the minister of defence, commander-in-chief, all the chief of staffs of different branches, the chief of staff of the reserve force, heads of the joint staff bureau – commanding officers of all but one of the brigades, down to battalion and company level, were Tutsi.[*] From 1996 nearly all the officers in important positions – including Paul Kagame, James Kabarebe (CO of the Republican Guard Brigade), Samuel Kanyemera, Patrick Kargeya (chief of the RPA intelligence department), Bosco Ntaganda, Kayumba Nyamwasa (CO 221st Brigade), and dozens of others – are known to have served with the NRA, most of them as top department, brigade and battalion commanders. At least as important was the fact that many of them received extensive, high-quality military training abroad. For example, before being appointed

---

[*] Mberabahizi blog: 'Ethnic Imbalance in the Rwandan Military and Security Organs: A Major Threat to Rwanda's Stability', 2 March 2011.

French paratroopers prepare their weaponry in front of a Douglas DC-8 transport at Kolwezi airfield, May 1978.
Photo French Ministry of Defence

Major Paul Kagame (right) with other participants at a military staff course at Fort Leavenworth, Kansas, 1990.
Photo Paul Kagame Collection

Table 3: Rwanda Patriotic Army, 1996–1997

Unit	Base	Area of responsibility
High Command Unit	Kigali	Directly assigned to the High Command
Republican Guard Brigade	Kigali	Kigali City Province
201st Brigade	Kibungo	Kibungo, Umatura and Byumba Prefectures
211th Brigade	Gisenyi	Gisenyi and Ruhengeri Prefectures
301st Brigade	Butare	Butare, Gikongoro and Cyangugu Prefectures
305th Brigade	Gitatama	Gitatama and Kibuye Prefectures
402nd Brigade	Kigali	Kigali and Kigali Rurale Prefecture

the commander of the RPA in 1990, Kagame underwent a course at the US Army Command and Staff College at Fort Leavenworth, Kansas in 1990.[*] Renowned for their brilliant tactics and thinking, key Rwandan officers were not only to dictate the following campaign and conclude it successfully, against all odds and expectations, but they remain the strongest element of the RPA today.

As of 1996, the RPA was actually an unknown military quantity in Central Africa. Carefully hidden from the public – not only by the government in Kigali that imposed strict control over the media, but also because of poor communications in eastern Zaire – its participation in the coming war remained unknown for the then foreseeable future. To a certain degree, this was convenient for the RPA. In mid-1996 it was still in the process of a build-up and not ready for a large-scale war. For many months after the start of the

First Congo War, it could not deploy more than three brigades of light infantry on the battlefield (including the 201st and 221st brigades), usually organized in battalion-sized task forces, supported by relatively few mine-resistant, ambush-protected vehicles (MRAPs), a few Toyota 4WDs and various trucks for transport. They were heavily dependent on logistic support provided by foreign PMCs in the guise of chartered civilian transport aircraft and helicopters.[†] Furthermore, while this force was used as a spearhead in all the major operations, a significant part of it had to be used to corset different insurgent contingents, and primarily deployed to secure occupied areas.

The RPA was busy building up the strength of its land forces during the period 1994–96, and thus dedicated relatively little attention in re-establishing an air force. In fact, serious efforts in this regard were launched only a few months before the outbreak of the First Congo War. Therefore, although capturing a miscellany of aircraft and helicopters of the former *Force Aérienne Rwandaise*, only one of these – a single Britten-Norman BN-2A Islander – remained operational. This aircraft was subsequently reinforced with several De Havilland DHC-4 Twin Otters, with which a single airlift squadron was established. Tasked with transport duties, this unit was to prove of crucial importance for resupplying rapidly advancing RPA troops deep inside Zaire (especially as these could otherwise not expect to receive any other kind of air support), in addition to a number of heavier civilian transport aircraft chartered from various foreign air freight companies.

Uganda People's Defence Force

Modern Uganda has a long and rich military tradition, dating back to 1902 when the Uganda Battalion of the King's African Rifles was raised in Britain's East African possessions. Except for performing both military and internal security functions within local British

---

[*] Kagame's course in Fort Leavenworth is downplayed because he only spent three out of a planned 12 months in the USA, before being forced to return and take over as commander of the RPA following Rwiyegma's death. However, Kagame himself acknowledged the importance of the training he received there, especially in information warfare and communications: "Central to my studies in Leavenworth [were] organization, tactics, strategy, building human resources, psy-ops, information, psychology and communication among the troops." See 'Dispatches from Disaster Zones, The Reporting of Humanitarian Emergencies,' conference paper by Nick Gowing, London, 27/28 May 1998.

[†] It is important to note the difference between mine-resistant, ambush-protected vehicles (e.g. MRAPs like the South African-made Casspir and RG-31 Nyala), armoured personnel carriers (e.g. Soviet-/Russian-made BTR-60) and infantry fighting vehicles (e.g. Soviet/Russian BMP-1/2). MRAPs are designed to carry the infantry from one point to the next, and offer reasonable protection from mines and small-arms fire. They are an element of motorized, not mechanized, infantry and cannot offer anything like the levels of protection that APCs offer. While able to offer fire support when properly deployed (e.g. in support of debussed infantry protecting them from RPG-type systems deployed by the infantry), they are not designed for deployment with the same purpose as the BMP-2 IFVs. Nevertheless, many armies around the world train their troops to use MRAPs the way they would APCs – often with poor results.

Paul Kagame (left) and James Kabarebe (behind Kagame's left shoulder, with beret), with a group of their officers.
Photo Inyenerine Collection

A matter of history. The days when the FAR used to operate a number of French-made transports and helicopters were all but over by 1996. When Kigali was captured by the RPA in July 1994, its sole Nord Noratlas transport – seen here in this photo from the 1970s – was flown out to Dar es Salaam IAP in Tanzania, and abandoned there.
Photo Pit Weinert Collection

James Kabarebe, here wearing the uniform of an RDF major-general, was the crucial aide to Paul Kagame, one of best Rwandan military commanders, and therefore appointed to command the combined Rwandan/ insurgent operations during the First Congo War.
Photo US DoD

colonies, this force saw external service in the First and Second World Wars. When Uganda was granted independence in October 1962, the Uganda Battalion formed the core of the newly established army. The situation changed in January 1964 when the British were asked to leave, following mutinies by several units demanding, among other things, nationalization of the officer corps and better pay. During the next few years Israeli military assistance became extensive and influential in the establishment of additional army units, the Police Air Wing and, shortly thereafter, the Ugandan Army Air Force in 1964. Under Israeli supervision, the Ugandan army developed into a strong, well-balanced and well-trained force during the second half of the 1960s, equipped with an affordable and useful mix of US, Italian, Soviet and Czechoslovakian equipment. Subsequently, the military influence in Ugandan politics increased considerably, culminating in the 1971 coup, after which the Israeli military mission was expelled. During a visit to Moscow by a Ugandan delegation in 1972, a large order was placed for MiG-21s, tanks, APCs, AAA pieces and assorted infantry weapons. Most of these were delivered between 1973 and 1975, at which time Soviet advisers were expelled from the country amid disagreements over the situation in Angola. The government in Kampala subsequently began antagonizing both Western powers and Israel, while simultaneously finding itself facing a major insurgency at home, which resulted in widespread destruction and thousands of victims. Under direct US threat, and in the face of an Israeli intervention that resulted in the destruction of a sizeable part of the air force in 1976, the government again approached Moscow and established close ties with Libya, where a number of Ugandan officers were sent for training. Finally, in 1978, Uganda provoked a war with Tanzania that resulted in the collapse of its military and the country's almost complete destruction.

During the early 1980s, a new military was established with US and British assistance, but this was subsequently weakened by ethnic divisions and a political struggle that only ended in 1986 when Museveni came to power. The emerging UPDF took on a different character from the NRA insurgency. While consisting of Museveni's young followers, it was augmented by fighters from the former Ugandan army and, by 1987, had grown in numbers and complexity, to where a divisional structure was introduced.

The UPDF lost much of its fighting capability and cohesion due to the desertion of the RPA cadre; the few successful offensives it fought during the early 1990s were soon overshadowed by the adverse publicity it received for its aggressive tactics and extensive human rights violations. Still, following the large-scale reorganization and retraining of many units, the army began recovering during 1992 and, by the mid-1990s, was further reinforced with financial aid from the USA, which enabled the provision of support by various Israeli arms dealers and PCMs. The Israeli company Silver Shadow (owned by Amos Golan) organized the acquisition of infantry weapons, MBTs, APCs and ammunition from the Ukraine while the British–South African–Ugandan-controlled PMC Saracen ran training courses for Ugandan officers and NCOs and mediated in a deal for the delivery of 70 Buffel and Casspir MRAPs from South Africa.

Under such circumstances, by 1996, the UPDF was capable of deploying and sustaining a substantial force on the border with Zaire. Controlled by its 2nd Division headquartered in Mbara (southwestern Uganda), this included the 17th, 69th, 73rd and 77th Infantry battalions, and was in the process of building up the Ruwenzori Mountain Alpine Battalion. During early 1997, the 2nd

This video still shows a South African-made Buffel MRAP in Ugandan People's Defence Force camouflage in the mid-1990s. Notable is the addition of Russian-made Dushka heavy machine guns.
Photo Mark Lepko Collection

The first of at least eight Mi-8MTV-2 delivered to Uganda in 1996.
Photo Kazan Helicopters

Division was reinforced with the addition of the 3rd Tank Battalion, equipped with T-55 MBTs. Overall, although primarily equipped with the same AK-47s, RPK and PKM machine guns, RPG-7s and light mortars like the RPA, an average UPDF infantry battalion was in possession of superior firepower and was more mobile.

By 1994, the UPDF began operating a small air wing – the Uganda People's Defence Force/Air Wing (UPDF/AW) – that numbered about 100 officers and other ranks and operated a miscellany of aircraft and helicopters. Beginning in 1995, this branch experienced a gradual expansion when three Agusta-Bell AB 206s and six AB 412s were purchased from Italy and, in 1996, when the first four Mi-8MTV-2s were ordered from Kazan Helicopters. Initially, it was the same ADCC – already active in Kigali, as described above – that recruited foreign pilots for these helicopters. However, over time, the ADCC also took care of training enough Ugandan pilots and ground crew to enable the UPDF/AW the purchase two Mi-172 Salon helicopters and increase the number of Mi-8MTVs to eight by 1998.

Most important for Ugandan military capabilities was the fact that the country was one of very few Central African nations with its own defence industry. For example, in the early 1990s, Saracen Uganda was originally established with Chinese and South African help, with the aim of launching the production of MRAPs and assembly of towed-guns of South African origin.

Furthermore, in 1995, an arms and ammunition factory – Luweero Industries, a wholly owned subsidiary of the National Enterprises Corporation – was established at Nakasangola. Two other arms factories were constructed thereafter, including one in Gulu, manufacturing light infantry armaments (this factory was devastated by insurgents in the mid-1990s but subsequently reconstructed). Due to the availability of such industry, Uganda later became capable of delivering armaments directly to allied insurgents in Zaire.[*]

Insurgent groups

ADF: Ugandan insurgents

The Allied Democratic Forces/Front (ADF) was established by exiles of different origin from central and eastern Uganda, primarily purist Mulims, said to have cooperated with the Lord's Resistance Army

(LRA) and another Ugandan insurgent group, the National Army for the Liberation of Uganda (NALU). The organization supposedly numbered 1,000 fighters, primarily armed with AK-47s, a few machine guns and even fewer mortars, and organized in companies of between 200 and 300 men, with very little coordination between them. Led by Ssentamu Kayiira, they operated out of the town of Kasindi, in northeastern Zaire, and were supported by the Sudanese Secret Service, which was providing them not only with arms and ammunition, but also training.

AFDL: the anti-Mobutu alliance

The origins of the most crucial insurgent organization in eastern Zaire in 1996 can be traced back to the first armed militias established by the Banyamulenge between 1991 and 1994, foremost of which was the Democratic People's Alliance (*Alliance Démocratique du Peuples*, ADP), led by Deogratias Bugera (also known as Deo or Douglas). The ADP was actually a very small organization of around 100 Zairian Tutsis, many of whom previously served with the RPA during the civil war in Rwanda, then returned to Zaire and obtained most of their armament by purchasing it from corrupt FAZ officers. Through 1995, the ADP underwent training in Rwanda – primarily by foreign PMCs, including Belgian national Willy Mallants, a former police official in the Belgian Congo in the 1950s, and later a communications engineer and colonel in the Belgian Army Reserve – and was reinforced by a number of RPA officers. By early 1996, it established a brigade of around 2,500 light infantry, armed with AK-47s, RPG-7s and 60mm mortars.[†]

Still, the ADP alone could not compare with the AFDL. On 18 October 1996, in Lemera (South Kivu), seemingly out of nowhere, a number of entirely unrelated insurgent organizations merged to establish an umbrella organization with the purpose of launching a full-scale war against Mobutu's government. Named the Alliance of Democratic Forces for the Liberation of Congo-Zaire (*Alliance des Forces Démocratiques pour la Libération du Congo-Zaire*, AFDLC or simply AFDL), this organization initially included four parties:

* New Vision, op cit, Xinhua, op cit and BBC Monitoring Service, op cit, 30 September 2003

† Koen Vlassenroot, *Citizenship, Identity Formation & Conflict in South Kivu: The Case of the Banyamulenge*, Review of African Political Economy, 2002, p. 508; Reyntjens, *The Great African War: Congo and Regional Geopolitics*, p. 48; and interview with former AFDL insurgent, provided on condition of anonymity, Paris, June 2009.

- The National Council of Resistance for Democracy (*Counseil National de Résistance pour la Démocratie*, CNRD), led by Kisase Ngandu, a Tetela from Kasai, was originally founded in 1991 and had around 300 fighters trained in Libya in 1990/91, then in Uganda in 1992 and finally in Rwanda in 1994.
- The *Mouvement Révolutionnaire pour la Libération du Zaire* (MRLZ), led by Anselme Masasu Nindaga, a Mushi from the Bukavu region and a veteran who fought with the in Rwanda in 1990–94.
- Bugera's ADP, which supposedly represented the Zairian Tutsis.
- Laurent Kabila's PRP, consisting of little more than a group of his aides and activists, some of whom had received military training in Uganda in 1994.

Kabila was promptly appointed the president of the AFDL, with Bugera as secretary-general, Ngandu as military commander and Nindanga as Ngandu's deputy.

The military strength of the AFDL at that time remains unknown, although it likely included the relatively well-trained and experienced core of the ADP and the CNRD. The AFDL was equipped only with AK-47s, a few machine guns and even fewer light mortars. They were unable to progress beyond a low-intensity guerrilla war as waged so often by so many parties in the history of Congo. However, there was no real need for them to grow in numbers as they had been established and organized by Kigali with the sole purpose of presenting the Rwandan invasion of Zaire as a Zairian insurgency. Its military wing was not only trained in Rwanda and Uganda, but was almost completely commanded by RPA officers, and while Ngandu was presented in public as its commander, the actual military commander was Colonel James Kabarebe, veteran of the NRA and RPA, close aide to Paul Kagame, former CO of the High Command Unit (HCU) and the Presidential Guard Brigade RPA.[*] For this purpose, the Rwandans and the AFDL began claiming that Kabarebe hailed from Rutshuru in North Kivu, although there is little doubt that he is a Banyarawanda raised in Uganda.

Although the AFDL was reinforced with around 10,000 fighters recruited in the Kivus and hurriedly trained at rudimentary infantry schools in Matere (North Kivu) and Remera (South Kivu), through early 1997 nearly all these were *Kadogo* (Swahili meaning 'short ones') – child soldiers with minimal military training and next to no value in combat (except as cannon fodder). Indeed, most of the units the AFDL could show in public, even in May 1997, only came into being in the days and weeks before, and never saw combat in the First Congo War.

Hutu organizations

While the mass of between 1.2 and 1.5 million Rwandan refugees that entered Zaire in 1994 consisted of innocent civilians who had fled their homes in fear of massacre, a relatively large group of Hutu extremists was among them. These included some 50 families of former government members, ex-FAR officers and Interhamwe leaders – most of whom found refuge in Bukavu – and around 16,000 other ex-FAR ranks with their families (around 80,000 people in all).

---

[*] The HCU was roughly similar in purpose to the Long-Range Reconnaissance Patrol of the US Army, a special forces unit employed on dangerous reconnaissance missions deep inside enemy territory.

Laurent Kabila inspecting one of the newly established AFDL units in Goma, April 1997. It was only with the help of foreign financial aid and contracts with various mining companies that the insurgents were able to purchase significant amounts of arms and equipment and establish large, well-equipped units like this one. Even then, such units did not become involved in any fighting before the last few weeks of the First Congo War. *Photo Mark Lepko Collection*

They were distributed within the camps with around 35,000–50,000 militants, with relatively few of them accompanied by their families. On crossing the border, the ex-FAR and Interhamwes surrendered some, but certainly not all their armament to the Zairian authorities. They handed over at least six AML-60 and AML-90 armoured cars, a few 120mm mortars and two Gazelle helicopters (the AMLs and Gazelles were returned to Rwanda in 1996), but kept their personal weapons, machine guns, grenades and tons of ammunition. Furthermore, they took with them most of Rwanda's hard currency reserves, thousands of vehicles and other public assets.

With the help of this money and equipment, and with the cooperation of the Zairian officers in charge of locally based FAZ units, and despite the presence of the UN and various NGOs, they soon began to exercise effective control over several genuine refugee camps, facilitating their control by organizing refugees into communes, distributing relief supplies, collecting taxes and generally keeping camp occupants in line.

However, the ex-FAR and Interhamwes did not manage to completely reorganize and rearm by the outbreak of the First Congo War. It was only during September 1996 that they began moulding the remnants of their organization to form the Party for the Liberation of Rwanda (PALiR) which, in turn, established its military wing, the Army for the Liberation of Rwanda (ALiR).

There is little doubt that at least some Hutu extremist leaders – foremost Jean Kambanda, former prime minister of Rwanda – began appearing in such refugee camps as the huge site in Mugunga, outside Goma, to make political speeches. Kambanda demonized the Tutsis and the RPF and warned the refugees against returning, claiming that anyone who did so was imprisoned or massacred. There is little doubt that the ex-FAR officers – who continued wearing their uniforms – gradually brought a number of refugee camps under their effective control and began exercising pressure upon those who expressed a desire to return to Rwanda. Dissent was dealt with through physical threat, and many of those who managed to escape the camps and return found that a price had been put on their heads, making them targets for the extremists. However, whether they could have launched

Scene from the huge Kibumba refugee camp in Bukavu, containing around 195,000 refugees. Representative of around 30 other sites in eastern Zaire, it was primarily occupied by Hutu civilians from Rwanda and Burundi, the vast majority of whom were in no way involved in the Rwandan Genocide. *Photo US DoD*

a major campaign to destroy the PRF government, bring a 'final victory' and 'definitive solution to the Hutu–Tutsi conflict', even if their military organization had been ready, is a matter of conjecture. Contrary to the official standpoint of Kigali, supposedly supported by documents captured in Mugunga camp in October 1996, the ALiR was not ready to launch a large-scale invasion of Rwanda.[*]

The extremists who created the PALiR were not the only political organization of Hutu refugees in Zaire and did not represent the majority. Quite the contrary, they were fiercely opposed by the more moderate RDR. Nevertheless, even the RDR came under attack from the new Kigali government and the PRF government began demonizing it as an organization of predominantly Hutu military officers and militia members bent on invading Rwanda. Furthermore, even once the ALiR was organized, it was not nearly as monolithic as many reports tended to indicate. It represented only that part of the former Hutu establishment that had found refuge in eastern Zaire. Its core included between 3,000–4,000 (UN sources) and 13,000–15,000 (Rwandan sources) armed men, primarily ex-FAR and Interhamwes who had taken part in the Rwandan Genocide. Headquartered in Kahuzi-Biega in Kivu, the ALiR was organized into two divisions, one headquartered in Beor/Douala, in North Kivu and the other in Arbre/Yaounde in South Kivu. These two divisional HQs operated a total of five brigades, headquartered in Limpopo and Tribune camps (outside

Masisi), Lilongwe (Walikale), Misissipi/Tensiometre (Shabunda), Kolwezi (Fizi) and Matadi (Kabambare).[†] The fighters of the ALiR were armed with AK-47s and RPGs, RPK medium machine guns, 60mm and 82mm mortars, anti-tank and anti-personnel mines, and light 12.7mm anti-aircraft machine guns. Furthermore, they were responsible for the maintenance of several 120mm mortars, various anti-aircraft guns and military trucks they had brought into Zaire, and which were stored in FAZ bases in Goma. Through clandestine acquisitions from Eastern Europe, they stockpiled ammunition, spare parts and fuel, sufficient for several weeks' intensive fighting.

FDD: Hutus from Burundi

Another group of armed Hutu refugees that emerged during the First Congo War consisted of exiles from Burundi. Named the Forces for the Defence of Democracy (*Forces pour la Défense de la Démocratie*, FDD), it was led by Pierre Nkurunziza and Jean-Bosco Ndayikengurukiye, and cooperated closely with the FAZ and ALiR, as well as various Mayi-Mayi militias.

The FDD totalled between 3,000 and 4,000 fighters, of which 1,000 were active in the Moliro, Mwenge and Moba areas, 2,000 between Fizi and Lake Tanganiyka and an additional 1,000 in the Lubumbashi area. They were equipped with the usual mix of AK-47 assault rifles, PKS and PKM machine guns, but had at their disposal sizeable numbers of 12.7mm and 14.5mm heavy machine guns, RPG-7s, and 60mm, 82mm and 107mm mortars. The FDD is also known to have used Motorola radio sets and satellite telephones, and operated speed boats on Lake Tanganyika.

---

[*] According to Kigali, after the RDF troops overran the FAZ base near the Mungunga camp outside Goma in November 1996, they captured documents indicating the ex-FAR and Interhamwes were trained by the FAZ in the use of heavy weapons and were preparing for an FAZ-supported counteroffensive to regain power in Rwanda.

[†] Herrmann, *Krieg, Ökonomie und Politik in Afrika*, p. 8

FNLC fighters with a captured FAZ truck. *Photo Mark Lepko Collection*

FNLC: Katangan Tigers and Angolans

Led by Nathanael Mbumba, the National Front for the Liberation of the Congo (*Front National pour la Libération du Congo*, FNLC) was an insurgent group established in the mid-1970s and centred round a group of former Katangan gendarmes – or Tigers – who found refuge in Angola and Zambia. In essence, the FNLC was actually an Angolan proxy group, maintained by Luanda for the purpose of intimidating the government in Zaire, in response to Mobutu's support for the insurgents of the National Union for the Total Independence of Angola (*Unioao Nacional para a Independencia Total de Angola*, UNITA) and, as of 1996, most of its members were descendants of former Tigers.

The FNLC's involvement in the First Congo War was two-fold. Part of the organization split during the early 1990s, when some of its members returned to Zaire. During the First Congo War many of them openly sided with Mobutu and even actively fought for the FAZ. A core of around 1,500 fighters, organized in two battalions, was deployed to fight on the AFDL's side, in February 1997, primarily armed with AK-47s and PKS machine guns, and a few light mortars. However, many Tigers resented the ADP – and thus the AFDL's ties with Tutsi-dominated Rwanda, and differences between these two organizations resulted in exchanges of fire.

More importantly, Mobutu's old rivalry with the government in Luanda eventually provoked a direct Angolan intervention. As soon as the Angolans realized the potential of the combined, RPA–AFDL force in February 1997, they decided to deploy not only two battalions of FNLC insurgents, but also at least two battle-hardened and South African-trained regiments of the Angolan Armed Forces (*Forças Armadas Angolanas*, FAA), including the 24th Regiment, well supported by artillery and armoured vehicles. The Angolan contingent was to play a crucial role during the final stages of the war, when its superior equipment enabled a rapid advance on Kinshasa.

Mayi-Mayi

As mentioned, the ethnic violence that spread through eastern Zaire in the first half of the 1990s prompted the emergence of a large number of different insurgent organizations and paramilitary forces. Two of these – the National Congolese Movement (*Mouvement National Congolais/Lumumbist*, MNC/L), led by Delphin Mulanda, and the Democratic Force for the Liberation of Congo-Kinshasa (*Forces Démocratiques pour la Liberation du Congo-Kinshasa*, FODELICO), led by the 1960s' rebel Antoine Gizenga – operated out of bases in Angola and Luanda and were active as deep within Zaire as the Ituri Forest and Kisangani area. However, the most widespread insurgent organizations were community-based militia groups formed to defend their local territory against any other armed groups, and generally known as Mayi-Mayi.

Most of these groups were run by local warlords, traditional tribal elders and village heads, and included relatively few politically motivated fighters. The majority of Mayi-Mayi fighters were illiterate and came from a tradition steeped in primitive animist beliefs. Many were promised immunity to bullets by witchdoctors and were told they would be transformed into *simbas* (Swahili for lions) when entering battle.

Generally, Mayi-Mayi militias were poorly armed. Some started off their insurgencies with only bows and arrows and spears. Initially, most Mayi-Mayi in North Kivu sided with the Rwandan-supported Banyamulenge insurgency because the Rwandan Hutu refugee camps were steadily encroaching on their lands. However, once the Hutus were forced to flee, the Mayi-Mayi began fearing Tutsi domination, and various Mayi-Mayi groups – primarily the Bembe militia, which represented different minor ethnic groups from the northwestern forests of Congo, who were always on the search for land to farm – allied themselves with the government in Kinshasa, receiving modern light infantry weapons of Western and Chinese origin. Other Mayi-Mayi groups sided with Hutu refugees, and at least two small groups reportedly cooperated with the Rwandan military, and thus came into possession of more modern arms of East European origin, even though most of these were still limited to light infantry weapons, primarily the omnipresent AK-47 and RPG-7.

CHAPTER THREE:
OPPOSING PLANS AND LOGISTICS

Such a simple comparison of the military forces involved, as provided in chapter 2, can never sufficiently explain the outcome of any armed conflict, especially not in the case of the First Congo War, where the relatively large and heavily armed FAZ was so severely defeated by a combined advance of the RPA, AFDL, UPDF and FAA. Furthermore, whether reinforced by the armed forces of several allied nations, the Rwandan military of 1996 should not have been in a condition to invade all of Zaire and defeat it in the fashion it did. Nevertheless, that is precisely what happened in the course of this war. The reasons for the success of the RPA are manifold and are to be found in a complex mix of factors that go beyond the condition of the FAZ in general.

Zaire: politicization and neglect of the military
Politicization of the military, decreasing funding and the resultant general neglect of duties, prevalent corruption and misuse of available resources and a heavy dependence on foreign advisers caused many problems within the FAZ and the FAZA. Different advisers not only advocated different military tactics – making even cooperation of two different battalions within the same brigade a difficult issue – but also caused the creation of different cliques within the military. Through the 1980s the officer corps grew to ridiculously large proportions, including no less than 50 generals and over 600 colonels. Their loyalties were divided between those trained in Belgium, the US or in France, in addition to tribal divisions, resulting in the formation of their own factions. Top ranks were from Equateur Province, but most of the officers that proved professional in the conduct of their duty or were from other areas, had either been purged ('mobbed') out of service or killed over the years, usually on the basis of little other than rumours about planning some sort of a coup against Mobutu. Due to their selection by loyalty instead of competence, most of the FAZ was run by ineffective leaders who lacked tactical and technical proficiency; they were so heavily corrupt that they actually weakened Mobutu's position. Instead of replacing or punishing them however, the Zairian president threatened, petulantly, to resign.

When, following the end of the Cold War, the US and France stopped their financial support for Mobutu, the government left all but a few privileged units to their own devices. Officers and other ranks of privileged units and agencies were paid, others not, resulting in much of the FAZ finding itself on the brink of collapse. The condition of even such units as the DSP, SARM and the Civil Guard soon deteriorated to a level where these were anything but a coherent military force. They resembled a group of armed cliques based on independent bodies, all gravitating around Mobutu. The FAZ remained loyal, at least on the surface; its officers, NCOs and soldiers tended to desert to signal their dissent, rather than involve themselves in plotting a coup.

Corruption and neglect, as well as a chaotic political and economic climate, and the relatively small amounts of arms and equipment purchased from a wide variety of sources, including the USA, France, Belgium, Italy and China, all combined to put the logistics system under heavy strain, until it all but collapsed. For example, Zaire purchased a total of 46 T-62 light tanks and 16 T-59 main battle tanks from China. Following their delivery, these MBTs were operated for several months, until they began breaking down due to a lack of maintenance. They were overhauled by a team of Chinese technicians, in 1985, but became inoperable again a few months after the Chinese left. The situation did not improve after another team of Chinese military advisers was assigned to the 1st Armoured Brigade in the mid-1990s, although the Chinese were well received by local officers and soldiers. By 1996, only 14 T-62s and 15 T-59s were considered as operational. Even the well-developed helicopter wing of the FAZA began showing effects of mismanagement, resulting in a situation where routine supply missions suffered as a result of the private commercial dealings of officers. The few remaining transport aircraft and helicopters were predominantly used for smuggling rather than for military support.

The wide variety of equipment purchased from different sources also resulted in very low fuel and ammunition stocks. Despite extensive stocks purchased from abroad and stored in major military facilities, units deployed in distant locations usually possessed very little ammunition and supplies. Due to the grossly neglected infrastructure and poor communications, they were unlikely to be replenished quickly, should the need arise.

In summary, the poor overall condition of the entire FAZ meant that even the elite units, like airborne and commando brigades, tailored to deploy swiftly from one part of the country to another when needed, became incapable of mobilizing rapidly, not to mention conducting the kind of operations for which they were established and trained. The FAZ's offensive capability, poor by any contemporary standards even before the 1990s, was practically non-existent by 1996, while defensive capabilities became limited to an absolute minimum. It had turned into a passive force, completely incapable of any kind of serious military operation in protection of the country, posing only a threat to the local population. Subsequent conduct of operations by the government in Kinshasa and the top Zairian military leadership have shown that there was neither interest, nor any kind of serious planning, for the kind of emergency that was about to break out. The only plan for a counteroffensive in eastern Zaire came into being once, what Kinshasa considered an insurgency, had already swept over most of the Kivus. Due to poor intelligence, it proved unrealistic and a case of too little and too late.

Rwanda and Uganda: uncertainty over objectives
Because of the lack of official documentation about the RPA's planning for the First Congo War, there is still much controversy over what exactly the Rwandan government and its military intended to achieve in Zaire in the latter part of 1996. Apparently, Kigali's involvement in Zaire was gradual. Rwandans first began providing arms, equipment and then training to Banyamulenge insurgents in order to enable them to protect themselves and fight the Hutu refugees. When this proved insufficient, the RPF decided to destroy the Hutu extremists and return the refugees to Rwanda, thus keeping them out of touch with the ex-FAR and Interhamwe. When this too proved insufficient,

Kigali launched an advance deep into Zaire, resulting in the spread of the insurgency that ultimately toppled Mobutu.

Upon closer investigation, it is hard to find evidence for this theory. Kigali was clearly instrumental in establishing and running the AFDL, reinforcing and corseting its various militias with RPA units, and running the campaign in eastern Zaire in its name. Rwandan planning only partially overlapped that of the Banyamulenge, and practically dictated to the leaders of the AFDL. Only a section of this organization came into being out of a need to protect the Banyamulenge from the government and various other ethnic groups. Although its members were trained in Rwanda and Uganda, and fought with the RPA until 1994, they were not related to Kigali's desire for the neutralization of Hutu extremists and a payback for the genocide of 1994. On the contrary, the Banyamulenge, recruited and trained by foreign PMCs and the RPA, were told they would fight to conquer the Kivus for Rwanda. Initial operations of the RPA inside Zaire were initiated as a result of the relatively successful reorganization of Hutu extremists which could have presented a potential threat in the future. But the campaign of pogroms against the Banyamulenge, launched by Zairian authorities, was a pretext rather than the actual reason for the Rwandan invasion. Furthermore, the Rwandan operation of returning the refugees was only partially successful and practically dictated the subsequent flow of the war. Namely, while approximately half of the refugees were forced back to Rwanda – and 'sorted out' in the process – most extremists managed to escape, proving that Rwandan control of the Kivus was insufficient.

The crucial issue of whether Kigali intended to remove Mobutu from the outset remains particularly controversial, even in the face of clear statements in this regard, including some by Kagame, provided to Western media after the First Congo War, but also by some US mercenaries who had supported RPA operations. Namely, mapping RPA operations indicates that the Rwandans were actively pursuing the refugees, thus the collapse of the FAZ and Zairian civilian authorities was a by-product of this operation. While there is little doubt that the RPA was well informed about the poor condition of the FAZ, it is doubtful whether the key Rwandan leaders assessed the toppling of Mobutu as within the reach of their military. Even once the Rwandan army was fully developed – a process that was still far from being realized as of mid-1996 – it would still be hopelessly out of condition to launch operations over near-intercontinental distances, defeat the quantitatively superior FAZ, and then establish control over a relatively small buffer zone in North and South Kivu, not to mention exercising control over a country the size of Western Europe, with a population nearly ten times larger than that of Rwanda. Similarly, it is certain that the initial Rwandan operations in the eastern Congo involved only two RPA brigades and did not follow a pattern that would indicate a plan for a campaign to conquer the whole of Zaire and reach Kinshasa. This changed only when Angola openly sided with the AFDL in February 1997, and when various Western leaders – primarily US President Clinton – began calling on Mobutu to step down which, in turn, confirms the theory that Kigali became interested in toppling Mobutu only once it realized that the FAZ was collapsing in the face of its advance in the direction of Kisangani.

For obvious reasons, it is unlikely that Kigali might publish related documentation any time soon and thus show whether Kagame ever asked for, and received, permission from the USA to topple Mobutu, as claimed by some. Official sources from both countries deny this. Data available from unofficial sources is unclear and, as

FAZ commandos about to emplane a DHC-5 Buffalo transport.
Photo Albert Grandolini

we are yet to see, France, a close US ally, was neither interested in a development of this kind, nor informed of these US intentions. Time and again through the mid-1990s, Kagame met US officials to discuss the situation in eastern Zaire, but he is not known for having advocated the removal of Mobutu. Instead, he usually warned of the threat to Rwanda emanating from the refugee camps, and that if the UN would not remove them, somebody else would have to do it. Apparently failing to prompt a US intervention, he decided to launch an invasion, using the principle of calculated risk that nobody would complain about Rwanda establishing a buffer zone between herself and the Hutu extremists, and that Mobutu's former allies would not return to protect him again.

In summary, this indicates that the immediate Rwandan aim was to exact revenge from the extremists and destroy their organization and fighting force, dismantle the refugee camps and remove their power base. A possible alternative, or a secondary aim, was to protect Rwanda and the Banyamulenge through the creation of a buffer zone along the border, perhaps with the overambitious and internationally unsupported aim of annexing portions of eastern Zaire, combined with returning the refugees in order to replenish Rwanda's depleted population and workforce.*

Under these circumstances, the military planning by the AFDL was of minor importance; that is, provided there was any such planning not dictated by Kigali. Undisputedly, some of the insurgent leaders intended to seize power in North and/or South Kivu; others might have dreamed about toppling Mobutu, but were hopelessly out of condition to do so – and all of them were heavily dependent on decision-makers in Rwanda.

Even less certain is the nature of Ugandan intentions and planning. Although Mobutu once supported the government of Tito Okello – before it was toppled by Museveni's NRA in 1986 – this was now history, and the president of Uganda was not directly at odds with the president of Zaire. Instead, busy fighting several armed opposition groups at home, and far from considering toppling Mobutu, Museveni suggested that the two governments cooperate with regard to possible oil exploration along their mutual border, in early 1996. Still, keeping

---

* Pasteur Bizimungu, president of Rwanda from 1994–2000, presented the then US ambassador in Kigali, Robert Gribbin, with the idea of a 'Greater Rwanda'. See Gribbin, *In the Aftermath of Genocide*, pp. 175-6.

Yoweri Museveni emerging from a Mi-172 saloon-helicopter of the UPDF/AW. What exactly his original intentions were in regard to Zaire in early 1996 remain unknown. *Photo Kazan Helicopters*

in mind Museveni's predilection for the Tutsi worldview, it is very likely that while Kampala originally intended little else but to deploy its forces in northeastern Zaire to fight the ADF, it eventually found it opportune to enter closer cooperation with Kigali and exploit the opportunity to grab some of the mineral wealth.

RPA's meagre resources

As mentioned previously, in 1996 the RPA was still in the process of reorganizing itself into a new national army. It must be kept in mind that this process was undertaken after a period of utter barbarism that ruined the entire country, uprooted more than half its population, and destroyed nearly all the elements of the state. As such, not only its military, but Rwanda as a whole, had to be rebuilt as a nation – and this under mind-boggling, challenging conditions.

Unsurprisingly, the RPA started with very little. Initially, soldiers assigned to the army, nowadays locally known as the Rwanda Land Forces (RLF), were primarily equipped with AK-47s, a small number of PKS, PKM and RPK machine guns and RPG-7 rocket-propelled grenades, a few light 60mm mortars and a few towed 107mm multiple-rocket launchers. During the course of the civil war, they captured a small amount of equipment from the former FAR, including some AML-60 and VBL APCs, perhaps 30 60-, 81-, 82- and 120mm mortars, several M2A1 (M101) 105mm howitzers and some of six D-30 122mm howitzers, delivered to the former FAR by Egypt in the early 1990s.

In September 1995, the RPA reportedly managed to snatch up no less than 64 armoured personnel carriers left behind by UN forces when they withdrew from Rwanda. The exact type of vehicles remains unknown. The small UN contingent deployed in Rwanda in 1994/95 and known to have been using APCs, was equipped with US-made M113s (Australians) and Russian-made BTR-60s (Ethiopians), but they took their vehicles with them when withdrawing. It is more likely that the reported APCs were actually miscellaneous 4WDs used by other UN contingents.

After the UN-imposed embargo on arms delivery to Rwanda was abrogated in 1995, Kigali was able to purchase arms from South Africa, including at least 20 RG-31 Nyala MRAPs. Oft-repeated reports about deliveries of 18 Buffel and 18 Casspir MRAPs, 81mm and 120mm

mortars and Belgian-made Blindicide 82mm anti-tank rockets, before 2002, cannot be independently verified, and there is no clear evidence of their deployment during the Second Congo War either.

In summary, the available equipment was far from sufficient to equip the type of army that the RPF leaders had in mind. On the contrary, many RPA units were short of weapons and equipment and, given how many troops it had to train and equip for its new units, and how many soldiers it had to resupply on the territorially huge battlefields of the First Congo War, it is actually surprising how much it managed to achieve during the conflict. Nevertheless, the Rwandan military units deployed during that war proved not only well trained and well led, but also highly effective, tough and a well-supplied and well-supported fighting force. This prompts the question of how this became possible, considering that Rwanda was, at the time, one of poorest countries in the world. Published data indicates an annual defence spending of less than US\$100 million. The answer lies in military aid from abroad, primarily from the USA, provided partially via official, but predominantly through unofficial, private channels, with help of various PMCs.*

US godfathers

Much has been published, and even more guessed, about possible and probable US involvement in the First Congo War on the Rwandan side. While there is little doubt that crucial members of the political and economic establishment in Washington, and especially within the Clinton administration, had clear interests in supporting Rwanda and a change of leadership in Kinshasa, the degree of US support for Kigali in the mid-1990s remains unclear; what is known about its official aspects is often overstated.

The first US military contingent arrived in Kigali on 30 July 1994 and consisted of 200 military personnel who established a civil-military operation centre that included a large USAF tactical airlift liaison and control element and military police detachment (for force protection), and various staff and logistic personnel. Additionally, two US Army officers (one assigned to the department of state and one to the office of the secretary of defence) and two special forces NCOs accompanied the US ambassador and staff to Kigali to re-establish the American embassy.

Initially, most US military activity in Rwanda was related to relief support and the establishment of relevant facilities, as well as the eradication of the consequences of the 1990-94 war. In January and February 1995, the US Army established a national demining office, training 120 RPA personnel in relevant operations. Furthermore, the DoD funded the operations of a US contractor, the Ronco Consulting Corporation, which eventually received a large demining contract, requesting it to remove more mines than had been laid during the previous war. Within the scope of the demining programme, the DoD provided relevant equipment, medical supplies, communications equipment and various other material to the RPA. Another US company, Haliburton, was contracted to construct Camp Mulindi,

---

* Researching covert programmes involving the use of PMCs for training and logistics support is particularly troubling. They are immune to Freedom of Information Act (FOIA) requests. Because of their proprietary status, PMCs also have a great deal of leeway to engage in covert activities far from the reach of any investigators. They tend to claim that their business is a protected trade secret and that the law is on their side and vice versa; when PMCs are involved, government officials can always deny any kind of direct involvement.

Three RPA soldiers with a UN peacekeeper in Gisenyi, following the rout of the FAR and Interhamwe in July 1994.
Photo John Isaac, unmultimedia.org

Abandoned matériel: machettes, bullets, magazines and an FAR helmet found in Gisenyi, July 1994.
Photo John Isaac, unmultimedia.org

Taken on the apron of Addis Ababa IAP, this shows a USAF C-5A Galaxy transport arriving to pick up BTR-60 APCs of the Ethiopian Battalion assigned to the UN contingent in Rwanda in 1994. Many of the vehicles deployed by the RPA during its initial advance into Zaire in October 1996 wore only poorly overpainted 'UN' titles on them, greatly adding to the confusion about their background, and the intentions of their occupants. *Photo US DoD*

One of the AML-60 armoured cars the RPA captured from the FAR in 1994. Very few of these remained operational by 1996, and nothing is known about their possible combat deployment during the First Congo War. *Photo US DoD*

which developed into one of the most important military training installations in Rwanda. This is where US advisers trained 30 soldiers of the HCU in July and August 1996, with emphasis on small unit leader training, tactical skills, land navigation, first aid and basic rifle marksmanship. Later, various US companies constructed additional military bases, such as Camp Gaviro (which became the home of the RDF Infantry School), Camp Kinigi and the Rwanda Military Academy in Gako.

Through 1995, partly as a result of their lack of action during the Rwandan Genocide, and partly through admiration, segments of the US department of defence gradually slipped deeper and deeper into cooperation with the RPA. Ably exploiting their position, the RPF leaders demanded – and which the Americans proved very happy to accommodate – relief aid, construction and reconstruction of military facilities and anything else that could be obtained with help of development loans granted to Rwanda by various international institutions (especially in light of the bitter 'economic medicine' imposed by the International Monetary Fund). Even so, the amount of money Kigali is known to have received from various sources during 1994–98 was insufficient to purchase all the arms known to have been delivered to Rwanda in the same period.

Instead, the Pentagon launched several training programmes that included the exchange of US Army and Rwandan officers and NCOs

and basic military training, but also far more, as summarized by US congressman Christopher Smith in the November 1997 hearing before the committee on international relations: "I also asked at the December 4 hearing whether we provided military training to the Rwandan armed forces ... A representative from the Department of Defense, Deputy Assistant Secretary Vincent Kern, said, 'I do not see any way that could possibly happen.' I was also assured that our military training of Rwandan forces deals 'almost exclusively with the human rights end of the spectrum, as distinct from purely military operations', and that we are talking about a 'kinder, softer, gentler side' of military training ... We have not provided the Rwandans with any of the sort of basic military training that you would get at Fort Bragg officer training or those sorts of things ... A few months later, it became clear that we had been providing Rwandan forces with training in a broad array of military skills, including psy-ops, tactical skills, and basic rifle marksmanship, whose connection to the human rights end of the spectrum is attenuated at best."

The Rwandans were actually less interested in classical military training; the leadership of the RPA included some of most

Kigali IAP with the US Army camp and communication equipment in the foreground. A USAF C-141 StarLifter transport (painted gunship grey) and a collection of civilian transport aircraft operated by different Rwandan and Russian cargo companies are also evident, September 1994. *Photo US DoD*

RPA NCOs at the Gako Academy, constructed with aid from the USA. Since 2005, more than 12,000 Rwandan NCOs have been trained at this facility alone. *Photo US DoD*

promulgate a message of national reconciliation.* In essence, the Americans taught the Rwandans how to manipulate public opinion and the media in regards to their military activities related to repatriation and other operations inside Zaire.

Except for providing financial aid and training, there are strong indications that US officials from the embassy in Kigali – and primarily the US military attaché there – travelled extensively to eastern Zaire, not only to actively monitor the development and deployment of the AFDL, but also to study the status of local FAZ units. The US defence attaché system is a long-term project run by the Defence Intelligence Agency (DIA). Furthermore, some of the US military staff deployed for the protection of the diplomatic staff in Zaire were reassigned to protect the US diplomatic staff assigned to the embassy in Kigali. Combined, this indicates the provision of US intelligence aid to Kigali as well. Related to the these trips were also probably operations by Lockheed P-3C Orions, which the US Navy is known to have run from Entebbe IAP during 1994–96. Although primarily designed and equipped with maritime patrol and anti-submarine capabilities, these aircraft are also potent reconnaissance platforms, equipped with powerful cameras and optical as well as electronic surveillance systems. Their task was further supported by reconnaissance satellites – even though the official standpoint of Washington, in regard to such assets until recently, was that these collected very little intelligence on developments in Rwanda and Zaire between 1994 and 1997, supposedly because of cloud cover. Still, various sources leave no doubt that the DIA would have provided the RPA commanders with precise satellite photographs to be used to detect ex-FAR and the FAZ concentrations.†

Rwandan logistics tail

For a military operation, undertaken by a country that lacks domestic production of armaments and ammunition, to be executed effectively, it requires not only a well-trained and -equipped army, but a strong, well-developed logistics tail, with an extensive network of required arms, ammunition and equipment resources, especially in the case

---

★ Summary: Report to Congress on US Military Activities in Rwanda, 1994–August 1997

experienced unconventional fighters in Africa in the early 1990s who could actually have taught the Americans a thing or two. Furthermore, if the US Army ever actually trained the Rwandans in "planning and conducting public information campaigns supporting refugee repatriation and reintegration" as officially stated by the Pentagon, this training – which coincidentally occurred only about two weeks before the mass repatriation of Rwandan refugees from Zaire – was either related to the planning of subsequent operations or was completely ineffective. Instead, the RPA was mostly keen on obtaining financial and material help from Washington, and elsewhere, to develop its public relations campaigns; this even more so once countries like the Netherlands had cancelled their assistance programme after the Kibeho massacre of April 1995, while Great Britain and other European donors threatened to 'reassess' the aid they were providing. From this aspect, it is unsurprising that some of the training provided by the US Army to the RPA in 1996 included such courses as mass refugee repatriation and the establishment of a public information capability at both national and local levels, to

† Whether the USN operated its more potent Lockheed P-3B Reef Point or P-3C Iron Clad reconnaissance aircraft over Rwanda and eastern Zaire, as claimed by several researchers (for example, see Wayne Madsen, *NewAfrican*, September 2001), remains unclear. Such aircraft – equipped with a comprehensive and sophisticated communication suite (including the then still rare and rather cumbersome satellite links), a communications intelligence suite, systems for acoustic recording and analysis, chemical detecting, and optical as well as infrared cameras – would have been especially useful for tracking down and even pinpointing leading ex-FAR and Interhamwe figures. However, their operations are always a well-protected secret and their presence in the area remains unconfirmed. Interestingly, instead of deploying their ELINT/SIGINT-gathering reconnaissance aircraft for tracking movements of Rwandan refugees, the British sent a single English Electric Canberra PR.Mk.9 photo-reconnaissance aircraft of No. 39 Squadron from RAF Marham to Entebbe, in Uganda, in 1996. The official task of this aircraft was to fly reconnaissance sorties over Zaire to gather as much information as possible on the numbers and movements of the refugees. A secondary task was to locate and photograph possible parachute drop zones in the event of an international humanitarian airlift (which ultimately proved 'unnecessary'). The Canberra in question (serialled XH169) flew an average of two sorties a day and returned to its base in the UK (via Cyprus) in early 1997; see 'Zaire Recce Mission', *Air Forces Monthly* magazine, February 1997.

The Pentagon ran, and still runs, various training programmes for the RPA land forces. Although officially said to be of a 'softer and gentler' nature, and – in more recent years – mainly related to the deployment of RPA units within the UN-led peacekeeping forces in Somalia, there are strong indications that many of these courses are important for developing other Rwandan capabilities, primarily related to propaganda warfare. Here a group of Rwandan troops is seen with a US adviser, 2010. *Photo US DoD*

of large-scale covert operations. This tail must depend on different sources so that should one of the sources be rendered incapable of delivering the necessary replenishment, another source can seamlessly fill the gap. In addition, it is easier to deny the existence of such a tail if there is more than one. In the case of Rwanda, it was an extensive network of political figures, businessmen and military leaders from around the world that enabled the military build-up. In the early 1990s, the massive armies of two major military blocs in Europe were disarming and vast amounts of armament, ammunition and equipment suddenly became available via official, but mostly unofficial channels. What also became available at the time was a large number of medium transport aircraft, primarily from the stocks of the former Warsaw Pact, but also a large number of cheap passenger airliners, withdrawn from service in the West for reasons essentially related to environmental protection. Together, the availability of armament and of cheap air transportation meant that Rwanda's backers were able to acquire, transfer and distribute the necessary equipment and supplies as and when necessary.

Deliveries of military aid to Rwanda during the second half of the 1990s are twofold. The more obvious, official aspect saw the involvement of USAF transport aircraft, as well as aircraft chartered by a number of US PMCs for hauling arms, principally purchased in Eastern Europe, to Kigali. The operations in question – including the massive Lockheed C-141B StarLifter and Lockheed C-5A Galaxy transports – were intensive enough to startle a number of observers who travelled to the area at that time.

Mobutu's national security adviser, Honore Ngbanda, was astonished to see the number of USAF transports at Entebbe and underway to Kigali, in early 1996: "When I saw the huge concentration of [the] US Air Force at Entebbe, where the situation rather resembled that of some major US military base than of any international airport, it became clear that the American military engagement stood in no relation to official statements about the reasons for US presence."[*]

The arms delivered in this fashion apparently ranged from between 20 and 24 T-55 MBTs, up to 40 BRDM-2 armoured reconnaissance cars, several batteries of D-30 122mm howitzers, MLRs of the same calibre, to at least 12 ZSU-23-4 Shilka self-propelled, radar-guided, quadruple anti-aircraft cannons and hundreds of Toyota 4WDs, most of which were subsequently equipped to serve as troop transports.

The gauntlet

No matter how intensive, the involvement of USAF aircraft in delivering military aid to Rwanda in 1995 and 1996 remained relatively

[*] Strizek, p. 240; deployment of USN P-3s was also reported by Madsen (p. 200), and first-hand sources interviewed by the author on condition of anonymity.

Although the Rwandans prefer to describe their operations inside Zaire (1996–97) as run entirely by their infantry units, the fact is that they deployed MBTs, APCs and other mechanized and motorized vehicles during this war, but, of these, there is very little pictorial evidence. This is a reconstruction of a Rwandan People's Army RG-31 Nyala MRAP as sighted in the Bukavu area in October 1996. Of interest is not only the four-colour camouflage pattern (including sand, red-brown, olive green and black) but also the unusual addition of the Soviet-/Russian-made DShK 12.7mm heavy machine gun.

Due to its poor mechanical condition and the lack of trained crews, FAZ armour saw next to no action during the First Congo War, and then primarily only in a fire-support rather than its intended role. This AML-60 was abandoned outside Kisingani during a clash with advancing Rwandan troops in March 1997. Notable is the licence plate – usually seen, not only on the FAZ, but also Rwandan AMLs – in the form of a square, painted in white, with digits stencilled in black.

The only part of the FAZ 1st (Independent) Armoured Brigade that saw any kind of action during the First Congo War was half a company of Type-62 light tanks, deployed by rail from Mbanza-Ngungu to the battlefield near the Nsele River Bridge, on 15 May 1997. Here, they were abandoned in the face of a rapid Angolan–Rwandan–AFDL advance. Photographs of FAZ T-62s from 1996 are rare, but it appears that they were painted in olive green overall. They were badly worn out and very dusty on their top surfaces and wore no identification markings.

Several UPDF infantry battalions deployed in Zaire during 1996 and 1997 are known to have included at least a company of either South African Buffel or Casspir MRAPs. Illustrated here is a Casspir, serial number T3724, painted olive green overall. Different from the South African vehicles, Ugandan Casspirs are usually armed with a PKM machine gun installed above the driver's cab and a PKT machine gun installed on the rear right corner of the troop compartment, above the rear doors.

A UPDF T-55 as seen in the Bumba area in early 1997. Painted in olive green overall, Ugandan tanks of this type differed very little from the Chinese-made Type-59s in Zairian service. The main difference was the turret numbers of the UPDF tanks; apparently these were based on the assignment of the tank to specific platoons and companies within the relevant tank battalion. Accordingly, 201 was probably the vehicle of the deputy commander of the 2nd Company, 3rd Tank Battalion, 2nd Division UPDF.

A reconstruction of the last FAZA SA-330C Puma sighted on several occasions in Kisingani and Kabalo in February and March 1997. Painted in green grey overall, it wore unusual roundels (without wings) on the rear fuselage, with the set of usual titles and its registration all applied in white.

The FAZA DHC-5D, registered as 9T-CBA, was apparently one of the last two airworthy examples of this type still in service in 1996 and 1997. Painted in a variant of the US Air Force's South East Asia camouflage pattern – tan (FS30219), light green (FS34102) and dark olive green (FS34079) on the top surfaces, and FS36622 on the bottom surfaces – the aircraft was reportedly deployed to support FAZ troops during operations related to the defence of Kisingani in late 1996/early 1997. It was often misused by several high-ranking Zairian officers for private purposes, primarily to haul loot, as well as for other nefarious purposes.

A reconstruction of the FAZA SA-316B Alouette III helicopter, coded 9T-HT10, found in derelict condition at Gbadolite in May 1997. The origins of this helicopter and the history of its service in Zaire remain unknown.

A reconstruction of one of the two An-26s delivered to Zaire from Serbia. The aircraft in question wore serials 71351 and 71352 before delivery, applied in small black digits on the rear fuselage, in front of the horizontal stabilizers, the last three numbers of which were repeated in white on the front fuselage. The aircraft is shown still wearing its original colours – dark sea grey (BS381C/638) and dark green (BS381C/641) on the top surfaces, and light blue on the bottom surfaces – but it is possible that it was at least partially repainted before the end of the First Congo War. All the former Serbian markings were crudely overpainted before delivery and it is unknown if any FAZA markings were applied instead.

A reconstruction of the FAZA J-21 Jastreb FG-483 shown armed with a FAB-250M54 bomb, used in the bombing of Shabunda and Walikale in early February 1997. The aircraft was operated in Zaire still wearing its original former Yugoslav and then the Serbian Air Force livery, consisting of RAF dark sea grey and dark green (BS381C/641) on top its surfaces, and light blue on the bottom surfaces. It had its former markings crudely overpainted with green. The serial FG-483 was a repeat of a serial worn earlier by one of the FAZA MB-326s.

A reconstruction of Tavernier's 'beans, bullets and gas-bomber' – the sole Hawker Siddeley Andover transport – based on recollections of eyewitnesses. Painted light grey overall and wearing no markings, this relatively rare, and thus quite auspicious, aircraft was used to supply the mercenaries of teams Alpha and Bravo during their deployment in eastern Zaire in early 1997. It was last seen at one of the airports in Kisingani shortly before that city was captured by the RPA in March 1997.

The Mi-35, coded 9T-HM2, was the second of four gunships of this type acquired by Mobutu's government with the intention of providing air support to Tavernier's mercenaries. Like the other examples, it was painted in beige and dark green on its top surfaces and sides and 'Russian light blue' (used extensively for Soviet aircraft and helicopters in the 1970s and 1980s) on the bottom surfaces. Except for the exotic mix of maintenance stencils and warning insignia in Russian, and the Zairian markings shown in this artwork, this helicopter might have received FAZA roundels on the rear fuselage where the old Soviet insignia was crudely overpainted, but there is no clear pictorial evidence for this.

A reconstruction of the westernmost MiG-21PFM, abandoned while still unassembled at Gbadolite in May 1997. The camouflage pattern was apparently based on the one tested by the former Yugoslav Air Force in the 1970s and consisted of the same Yugoslav equivalents for dark sea grey and dark green on the upper surfaces, and 'Russian light blue' on the bottom surfaces. The exact camouflage pattern on the rear fuselage and on the fin remains unknown.

A reconstruction of one of the UPDF/AW's Mi-8MTV-2s known to have been operated during 1996/97, but not seen since. Notable is the disruptive camouflage pattern in two shades of green, the addition of exhaust diffusers over the engine outlets, and four chaff dispensers under the boom, as well as the use of UV-32-57 pods for unguided 57mm rockets – perhaps from surplus Ugandan MiG-21 stock left over from the 1970s – instead of the more common B-8V pods with 80mm rockets.

Zairian flag as seen on FAZ aircraft and vehicles

Official flag of Rwanda, 1962–2001

Flag of the ALiR

Flag of the AFDL

Official crest of the Zairian Armed Forces

Official crest of the Rwandan Defence Force

Flag of the Katangan Gendarmerie

Flag of the UPDF

Top: French paratroopers waiting to collect foreigners from Kigali for evacuation via the local airport in April 1994.
Photo Pellizzari Xavier/Savriacouty Claude, ECPA-ECPAD

Above: Thousands of refugees who did not manage to leave Rwanda before the country came under RPF/RPA control, gathered in huge camps like this one at Gikongoro during July 1994. They were repeatedly abused by Hutu extremists and found no sympathy or understanding from the RPA insurgents who generally considered anybody fleeing as doing so because they were guilty of genocide.
Photo John Isaac, unmultimedia.org

Left: A graphic depiction of the plight many Rwandans suffered in 1994. After the genocide of the Tutsis and moderate Hutus at the hands of extremist Hutus, a mass of Hutu civilians fled their homes, fearing retaliation by the RPA. In addition to dying at the hands of Tutsi insurgents and Hutu extremists, thousands died of malnutrition and exhaustion. Over 50,000 died as a result of a cholera outbreak in October 1994. *Photo US DoD*

Masses of Rwandan people, primarily Hutu, uprooted because of the civil war and genocide, fled to neighbouring countries. This group was photographed by US Army troops involved in efforts to provide fresh water to the refugees in October 1994. *Photo US DoD*

Throughout 1994 and 1995, Western powers continued sending relief aid to Rwanda, paying little attention at an entirely new set of dynamics, which would soon to spill over into neighbouring Zaire. Here, a column of US Army trucks loaded with water for refugees, is underway in Rwanda, late 1994. *Photo US DoD*

Two SF.260MC trainers as seen at Kamina Air Base, shortly after their delivery in 1971. Zaire later ordered an additional 12 of these during the 1970s, but less than 20 remained intact and all were stored by 1990. *Photo Aermacchi*

This was one of the first three MB.326s delivered in 1969. Except for wearing a disruptive camouflage pattern in tan (FS30219), olive green (FS34102) and dark olive green (FS34079), these aircraft initially had the outsides of their wing-tip tanks, as well as tops of the fin, painted in bright red. Notable is the old Congolese fin-flash, replaced by the FAZA flag shortly after delivery. *Photo Aermacchi*

The first two-seat Mirage 5DM (serial M201) built for Zaire, photographed shortly before delivery. Most of the FAZA Mirages were operational for fewer than ten years. *Photo Tom Cooper Collection*

The FAZA Hercules fleet saw intense service in the 1970s but subsequently fell into disrepair. This was one of two Zairian C-130Hs that survived long enough to be sent to France for major overhaul in 1996. *Photo Tom Cooper Collection*

A column of Rwandan troops, recognizable by their rubber boots and a mix of folding-stock and fixed-stock AK-47s. *Photo Mark Lepko Collection*

Two Ugandan T-55s outside Bumba on the Congo River during the later stages of the First Congo War. Most of these tanks were purchased through Israeli agents via Belarus and required comprehensive overhaul before the UPDF could deploy them in combat.
Photo Pit Weinert Collection

Although the AFDL leaders did much to present their military forces as well-trained and -organized outfits, the majority of troops were *kadogos*, or child-soldiers, recruited by Anselme Masasu Nindaga. They had minimal military training and were of little value in combat. They were only organized into units between January and May 1997. The boys shown here here display their AK-47s and PKM machine guns.
Photo Mark Lepko Collection

FAR soldiers, with a Dushka heavy machine gun of Soviet/Russian origin, seen battling the RPA outside Kigali, 12 June 1994. They kept their uniforms and most of their sidearms after escaping to Zaire. *Photo Mark Lepko Collection*

Community-based militia groups, generally known as *Mayi-Mayi*, have rich traditions in the Congo. Originally organized by tribal elders or village heads, during the 1980s and 1990s many of these were established by warlords with their own commercial and political interests. Poorly equipped earlier on – as illustrated by this group of Bangadi *Mayi-Mayi* armed with old hunting rifles and sticks – they were to develop into a potent fighting force during the Second Congo War. *Photo Finbarr O'Reilly*

A group of DSP troops on a French-made VLRA 4x4 truck. Although one of the few privileged military units, even they were frequently not paid for lengthy periods and often found no other solution but to loot in order to survive. The terror they spread during 1990–96 caused many Zairians to consider the Rwandan invasion, and the appearance of the AFDL insurgents, as a form of liberation. *Photo Albert Grandolini Collection*

Although reorganized as Rwanda's official military in 1996, the RPA was still very much a guerrilla force, consisting predominantly of light infantry, primarily armed with AK-47 assault rifles. The number of available RPK and PKM machine guns was very low and even 60mm mortars were scarce. *Photo unmultimedia.org*

ALiR fighter in the jungle of South Kivu. *Photo Finbarr O'Reilly*

The town of Goma in northern Kivu, only a few kilometres from the Rwandan border, was the scene of a major RPA attack on local FAZ units, with a number of huge refugee camps nearby. *Photo Guido Potters*

Over a million Rwandans, primarily Hutus, fled to eastern Zaire during 1994–96, where thousands died of malnutrition, exhaustion and epidemics, even before the camps came under the control of Hutu extremists. Here an FAZ truck drives by the bodies of refugees who died from cholera in the camps in the Goma area, July 1994. *Photo unmultimedia.org*

The huge Kibumba camp outside Bukavu was populated by around 195,000 registered refugees. Protected by a single Zairian DSP company and one camp security battalion, it was swiftly overrun by the RPA on 29 October. *Photo US DoD*

Rwandan operations during the first few months of the invasion of Zaire, September 1996-February 1997.

Top right: The rugged terrain of the Kivus and lack of land communications created immense logistical problems for the combined RPA/AFDL/UPDF advance. Because of this, the availability of various local airfields and landing strips, and the capability of Rwandan troops to capture and secure these, practically dictated the direction and pace of the advance. Rwandan planners were constantly in search of suitable, secure sites where they could resupply their advancing units. The fall of large cities with several airfields – Kisingani in particular – was therefore a major achievement that bolstered the RPA's ability to continue its advance. *Photo Guido Potters*

Right: An RPA soldier, seen in North Kivu, armed with a folding-stock AK-47 and wearing the characteristic rubber boots. *Photo Mark Lepko Collection*

One of the refugee camps outside Goma, July 1994. The effects of mortar and artillery fire deployed against such a hopelessly overcrowded area were devastating. *Photo John Isaac, unmultimedia.org*

One of the FAZA's last operational SA-330B Pumas (serial 9T-HP18) was sighted several times landing in the Amisi camp to deliver arms and ammunition to ALiR fighters. Its subsequent fate is unknown but it was probably abandoned at Kindu airport. *Photo Mark Lepko Collection*

US Navy technicians maintain the main radar on a P-3C Orion maritime patrol aircraft of the VP-16 Squadron at Entebbe IAP, November 1996. With high-tech equipment, a maximum range of 7,400km and endurance of ten hours, they were prefect platforms to track the movement of the refugees – and no doubt the ex-FAR and Interhamwe – around eastern Zaire. *Photo US DoD*

Externally, the P-3 Reef Point (as they were called until 1997, when the designation 'Iron Clad' emerged) is not dissimilar to the standard P-3C Orion maritime patrol aircraft, which means that they were fairly inauspicious. The US Navy's VP-10 Reef Point/Iron Clad aircraft are known to have worn markings of various other squadrons to mask their actual purpose, the major difference being a flat window behind the cockpit for optical surveillance equipment, instead of the usual observation blister. *Photo US DoD*

Taken by USN's P-3, this photo shows a column of Rwandan refugees in the Goma area in November 1994. *Photo US DoD*

limited in scope. In fact, most of the arms shipments reached Kigali aboard chartered civilian air freighters. Curiously, it seems that in this regard the RPF leadership and its US backers followed the example of the extremist Hutus. On 25 May 1994, a Nigerian-registered Boeing 707 (5N-OCL), operated by Overnight Cargo Nigeria, took off from Ostend airport in Belgium, carrying 39 tons of small arms and ammunition and one passenger, Mr T. Bagosera. The plane landed in Goma where the load was taken over by FAR officers. Bagosera was actually Colonel Thóneste Bagosora, a top FAR official and one of the main organizers of the Rwandan Genocide.

Barely a month later, another aircraft – this time registered in Liberia and flown by a Belgian crew – took off from Ostend to pick up arms in Libya (including light artillery pieces, rifles and ammunition), and delivered them to Goma as well.* Once in Zaire, the arms in question were loaded onto a convoy of FAZ trucks and, escorted by Bagosora, transported to Rwanda.

A subsequent UN inquiry revealed that these arms were purchased by ex-FAR leaders from Ronald Desmet, a Belgian businessman, who shipped no less but 150 tons of arms to Goma and Uvira by air between February and May 1996. It was in this fashion that the practice developed of using Ostend airport as a base for a number of companies to provide transport aircraft to other companies without taking any responsibility for the cargo or its destination. Operating out of Ostend, the aircraft in question proved easily capable of collecting arms from various European suppliers and flying them to wherever they were needed in Africa.

Clandestinely landing heavy transport aircraft with illicit cargo in war time, while simultaneously breaking international embargoes, requires cooperation from more than just a few individuals. It takes internationally organized networks of well-funded and well-connected individuals, *au fait* with brokering and logistics, and with the ability to move illicit cargo round the world without raising suspicion, and who, at the same time, can slickly deal with the daily technical and bureaucratic obstacles. The Americans obviously found such people and within a relatively short period of time, two prominent air freight companies based in Ostend emerged: Sky Air, run by Pakistani Sayed Naqvi, and Seagreen, owned by two US citizens, David Paul Tokoph and his brother Gary, who later acquired the bankrupt Zambian national airline and privatized it as Aero Zambia. Their aircraft usually collected arms and ammunition sold by Kintex from Burgas, in Bulgaria, and hauled these primarily to Rwanda. Sky Air's Boeing 707, registered in Liberia as EL-JNS, is known to have flown no less than 25 loads of Kalashnikovs and ammunition from Bulgaria to Rwanda in 1997 alone and, in 1998, it was also sighted at Otopeni IAP, outside Bucharest, Romania. One of the pilots flying B707s was a Briton who recalled:

"This job does require crews with considerable experience, due to the problems that are encountered when carrying unpleasant cargo. Lack of overflight clearance can make things difficult as delays are unacceptable due to the bank drafts used to pay for the equipment having a short life, i.e., the stuff must arrive within a given time. The boss may tell us that we are OK across Iran, the UAE and Oman for instance, but with no further clearance into Africa. This means 'disappearing' for a while and 'reappearing' on approach to the destination, to land and possibly be met by a former Soviet bloc agent

---

* *Rearming with Impunity*, HRW, May 1995

A C-130H of the US Air National Guard rolling down a taxiway at Entebbe IAP. The intensity of US military traffic through Entebbe and Kigali in 1995/96 was certainly a surprising sight to many observers. *Photo US DoD*

Two C-130Hs – the one in foreground belongs to the Royal Canadian Air Force, the one in the background is operated by the USAF – share the apron at Entebbe IAP with an Antonov An-12 chartered by the UN from Russia. *Photo US DoD*

USAF C-130H crews on the tarmac at Kigali IAP. While earlier, much activity was related to the delivery of relief aid, or rather 'routine, peacetime operations', to various military contingents deployed to Rwanda under UN supervision, in time not a few of these flights were delivering armaments to the RPA, and purchased in Eastern Europe. *Photo US DoD*

The original gun-runner, the Boeing 707 5N-OCL, operated by Overnight Cargo Nigeria, was used to deliver arms shipments to ex-FAR and Interhamwe in Goma,1994. *Photo Jan Laporte*

with impeccable English and good contacts ... A lot of this sort of flying goes on and we sometimes saw unreported aircraft silently crossing our track. It is hardly surprising given the astronomical sums of money involved and, indeed, our own national interests."

Apart from flying between Europe and Africa, in some cases the B707s loaded arms at Entebbe in Uganda, and delivered them to Kigali:

"The freight was loaded at the old terminal, connected to the new one by taxiways. The military controlled the old terminal and the buildings were just as the Israeli commandos left them in 1976 – wrecked."

However, none of the air transportation companies involved in the flourishing business of arms trafficking through Central Africa in the 1990s became as famous, or notorious, as the conglomerate of companies run by Victor Bout, a Tajik, with Russian and Ukrainian passports and several others to boot. This former officer of the Soviet Air Force, a graduate from the Foreign Language Section of the Moscow Military Academy, once served with a Soviet transport regiment, hauling cargo all over Africa, but primarily to Mozambique in the 1980s. After the unit was disbanded, in 1991, he remained in Africa and began setting up his own air cargo business, drawing on his vast knowledge of local conditions and contacts. With the help

of his connections – the people in control of the better part of the ex-Soviet arsenal left behind in Belarus and the Ukraine after the end of the Cold War – Bout was in a perfect position to develop a fully operational system, clandestinely transporting arms, money and people. He also proved able to find and recruit pilots capable and ready to fly anywhere, and authorities happy to issue the so-called end-user certificates – crucial documents issued by authorities of countries not under arms embargo. Indeed, the ability to easily obtain end-user certificates was what made the difference between Bout and his competitors, like Naqvi or the Tokoph brothers. This meant that his aircraft could load any cargo, regardless of its origin, and deliver it wherever needed. Once his aircraft reached what became known as 'The Gauntlet' – a vast and virtually uncontrolled airspace, stretching from the southern Sahara Desert south to the Limpopo River, and not covered by any kind of air traffic control (ATC) or military radar surveillance – became Bout's playground, and he could divert to any destination necessary, as explained by the same British B707-pilot as cited above:

"'Disappearing' means turning everything off and climbing to an unused level such as 34,000–36,000 feet ... the importance of this is we were turning off any sources of electromagnetic emissions in order to make us 'invisible', then being invisible means being 'safe'."

This Ostend-based B707 (N21AZ) operated by Seagreen Air Transport was also used to haul weapons to Rwanda. *Photo Jan Laporte*

Victor Bout, or Butt, or Bhutt, whichever suited at the time. *Photo Mark Lepko Collection*

Officially based in Sharjah, in the United Arab Emirates, this Antonov An-8 (registration EL-AKZ) was operated by Air Cess and was frequently sighted at Kigali IAP in 1996/97. *Photo Richard Vandervord*

Barely a year after leaving military service, Bout was already in a position to purchase three Antonov transports and establish a company in Sharjah, UAE. In 1995, he then surfaced in Ostend, to set up the Trans Aviation Network Group company (TAN), with Michael-Victor Tomas from France, and Ronald de Smet from Belgium (a son of a former official of the Gecamines Company).

In regard to Zaire, through 1995 and 1996, aircraft operated by various Bout companies out of Ostende were mainly providing services to the government in Kinshasa. However, he simultaneously established the company Cessavia, later Air Cess Rwanda, and then the Air Cess Equatorial Guinea, Air Cess Holdings Ltd., Air Cess Inc., and Air Cess Miami (registered in Miami, Florida, USA), then Air Cess Liberia, Air Cess Swaziland (Pty.) Ltd., Air Pas, Air Pass, CES-AVIA, Chess Air Group, or Pietersburg Aviation Services & Systems – all of which were registered in Malabo, Equatorial Guinea, but had their official office as P.O. Box 3962 or 7837, Sharjah, United Arab Emirates, or Islamabad, Pakistan, or Entebbe, Uganda.

As absurd as it might sound, through the late 1990s, Bout operated at least four different companies based in countries directly involved in the Congo/Zaire and at war with each other, including Bukavu Aviation Transport (based in Burundi), Business Air Services (Congo/Zaire), Great Lakes Business Company (GLBC, based in Goma) and Okapi Air (Uganda). This complex network of companies with a large volume of transiting cargo, thanks to the use of some

20 different transport aircraft of Russian origin, but also bank secrecy laws and bustling free trade zones of the UAE, made Bout's companies a perfect partner for clandestine arms deliveries to Rwanda and eastern Congo. Unsurprisingly, Bout's aircraft were to see heavy involvement – primarily on the Rwandan side – in both the First and the Second Congo Wars.

Unofficial but able

This is not to say that the ex-FAR and Hutu militias failed to continue using similar channels for the acquisition of arms. Despite a set of UN embargoes, using their old links to France, members of the former Hutu-dominated Rwandan government began purchasing arms while withdrawing to Zaire in July 1994, when at least one shipment to Goma is known to have taken place. While Paris officially denied any kind of involvement, some French officials justified such deliveries as the fulfilment of contracts negotiated with the Rwandan government before the embargo was in place. Subsequently, embargo-busting activity was greatly facilitated by the Zairian authorities, some of whom not only delivered arms directly, but also helped the Hutus with acquisitions from abroad, sometimes with help of FAZ-contracted private companies, or with the help of chartered foreign transport aircraft, and, of course, at all times facilitated by Zairian end-user certificates.

This military build-up was possible because a) the former Rwandan government brought with it all Rwanda's hard currency and foreign assets, and b) the extremists imposed war taxes on the refugee community, began selling relief goods illegally and launched a major fundraising avenue in Kenya.

Reportedly, additional funding was obtained through drug and arms smuggling, primarily through channels established by South Africa during the Cold War to circumvent the UN arms embargo imposed on that country between 1977 and 1994, as well as channels used to support the UNITA insurgency in Angola, and those used to smuggle arms from Western Europe and the USA to Iran during the 1980s.

During the first months of 1995, ten–12 planeloads of arms for the ex-FAR and Interhamwe were delivered by chartered Ilyushin Il-76 transports from Bulgaria to Goma, while two aircraft registered in the Ukraine brought additional arms from the former Yugoslavia. Later the same year, the Hutu established contacts with China, which delivered a consignment of AK-47s and RPG-7s, justifying the sale

Lt-Gen Salim Saleh, half-brother of Ugandan President Museveni and UPDF chief-of-staff. Saleh was crucial for turning the Ugandan intervention in Zaire into a commercial enterprise – with near-catastrophic consequences for the war-fighting capability of the entire army.
Photo Mark Lepko Collection

by stating that there was no embargo in place against Zaire.* Even a company with British–Israeli connections, the Mil-Tec Corporation (registered in the Isle of Man) brokered a deal for the delivery of mortars, automatic rifles and artillery shells from Albania and Israel to Goma. Such activity continued through 1996, with three aircraft hauling a total of 150 tons of ammunition to Goma and Bukavu in February, March and May of that year.

★ *Africa Confidential* reported in 1995 that Agathe Kazinga, Habyarimana's widow, accompanied Mobutu on his trip to China in late 1994, and allegedly exploited this opportunity to purchase arms for the ex-FAR.

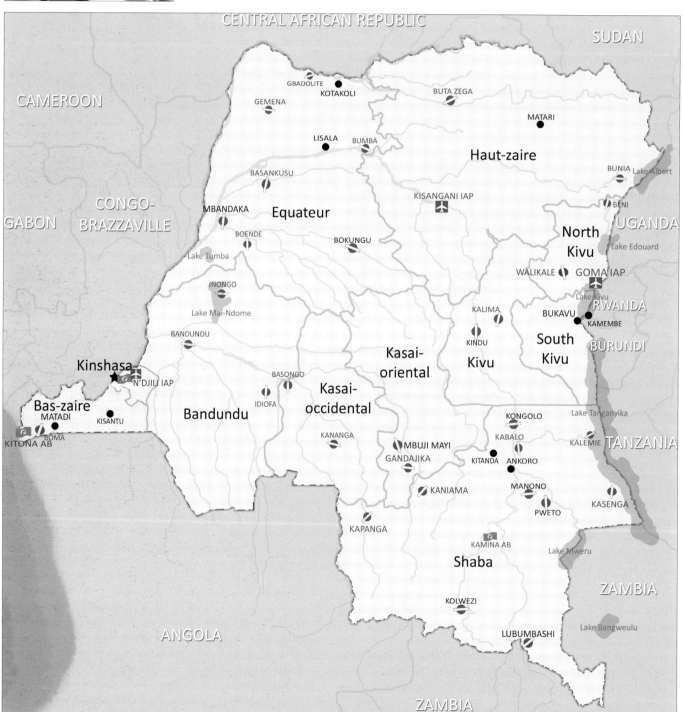

Availability of a large number of airports and airfields across Zaire, as well as widespread corruption and disfunctional authorities, meant that poor land communications could be replaced by the use of transport aviation, but also that any party with the necessary funding could order deliveries of arms shipments straight into its own backyard. This map shows only the 30 most important air bases, airports and airfields in Zaire in the mid-1990s.

CHAPTER FOUR:
THE FIRST CONGO WAR

While often described as the Banyamulenge problem, and then as an insurgency, the root for the outbreak of military operations during the First Congo War lies in an RPA operation into the eastern parts of North and South Kivu. When this failed to attain its goals, in spite of easily defeating locally deployed FAZ units, the Rwandans gradually expanded their aims: 1) destroying the ex-FAR and Interhamwe extremists and repatriating, or massacring, the mass of Hutu refugees in the Kivu to establishing a buffer zone along their border with Zaire, 2) bringing major sources of mineral wealth in this area under their control, and 3) advancing in the direction of Kisangani and Kindu, combining this enterprise with their pursuit of surviving Hutu extremists and the refugees. Under these auspices, the RPA's role in the war was crucial, while the AFDL 'insurgency' as such mattered very little, and actually proved to be nothing else but the 'beefing up' of deployed Rwandan units – even more necessary because the advance deeper into Zaire required far more troops than originally deployed. Eventually, the Rwandan advance on Kisangani, and then the involvement of Uganda and Angola, transformed the First Congo War into a kind of classic military campaign, in which logistics, transportation and firepower played increasingly dominant roles.

Early Rwandan infiltrations

Direct involvement of RPA units in Zaire began in 1995 when members of the HCU made their first forays deep into that country in their search for leading Hutu extremists, primarily top ex-FAR commanders and Interhamwe militiamen. The extremists were hard at work reorganizing and recruiting new fighters, but also purchasing arms abroad and rearming themselves. Some of their leaders were calling for a counteroffensive into Rwanda. However, it remains unclear if they indeed planned a viable operation, as claimed by Kigali. Considering the build-up of the RPA and the amount of support Rwanda was receiving from abroad, they could not have expected any such operation to succeed, as the amount of armament they received between 1994 and 1996 was hopelessly insufficient. Nevertheless, whether driven by its own or US interests in securing Congolese mineral resources, or its wish for retribution for the 1994 genocide, Kigali was not keen to let them improve their capabilities. During July and August 1996, Rwandans began infiltrating around 200 ADP fighters, supposedly led by Laurent Kabila's son, Joseph, into the mountains of North Kivu, followed by 1,000 others, led by Nganda, who infiltrated South Kivu, while the RPA deployed four or five battalions with around 5,000 troops, supported by mortars, MLRSs and heavy artillery along the border with Zaire, primarily opposite Goma and Bukavu.*

---

* Curiously, Kigali officially maintains that the RPA deployed only two battalions of own troops during the first phase of the First Congo War, namely the 3rd Battalion in the Goma area and the 101st Battalion in the Bukavu–Uvira area. Considering the size and the terrain/battlefield, not to mention the number of refugees they intended to coral and then forcefully return to Rwanda – almost 2 million according to official Kigali figures – and about an equivalent of six brigades of FAZ and ALiR troops present in the Kivus, these 1,200–2,000 troops would be hopelessly insufficient for the task at hand.

Although reorganized as Rwanda's official military in 1996, the RPA was still very much a guerrilla force at the outset, predominantly consisting of light infantry, primarily armed with AK-47 assault rifles. The number of available RPK and PKM machine guns was very low, and even 60mm mortars were scarce. *Photo unmultimedia.org*

The first RPA commandos sent to support the Banyamulenge were infiltrated during the night of 31 August/1 September from Cibitoke in Burundi, but this attempt had an unfortunate start as the unit in question clashed with the FAZ at Businga, losing three men.

The FAZ forces facing the Rwandans and Banyamulenge actually comprised an ineffective conglomerate of units. The Goma area was secured by two battalions of camp security forces (well paid by the UN, but led by corrupt DSP officers), a battalion from the 31st Parachute Brigade, one battalion of Civil Guard and an SARM company. The Bukavu area was secured by a battalion of camp security forces, one battalion from the 31st Parachute Brigade and another SARM company. Of course, the FAZ could count on support from the camp security forces and well-armed Hutu militants, but most of these were busy building up the ALiR – which in turn was the stated reason for the RPA deployment. Indeed, when Kagame visited Washington in August 1996, he warned the USA that the international community was not only ignorant of the persecution of the Banyamulenge in eastern Zaire, but was in fact aiding the perpetrators of the 1994 genocide by providing relief aid to Hutu refugees and hiding the murderers among the innocent. Furthermore, he said that he would take military action against the camps and the Mobutu regime if this intolerable situation continued. Kagame came back from the USA around the time Banyamulenge civilians began showing up at the Rwandan border, with tales of terror and massacre.

For example, in early September, the governor of South Kivu, Lwasi Ngabo Lwabanji, and his commissar in Uvira, Shweba Mutabazi, ordered all Banyamulenge to leave the country within a week or face harsh consequences. Those who would not leave would be declared outlaws. Without waiting for the ultimatum to

The RPA made extensive use of infiltration tactics during the early stages of the First Congo War. These two Rwandan youngsters wait for the signal to attack. *Photo Albert Grandolini Collection*

expire, the Bembe and Barega militias, supported by the FAZ, began attacking Banyamulenge villages in South Kivu, killing and raping, forcing survivors to flee to Rwanda. Between 9 and 30 September at least five villages in the Bukavu area were attacked and up to 200 Banyamulenge were massacred. In the process of this operation, FAZ units clashed several times with unidentified armed elements near the Lemera village north of Uvira. However, they neither recognized the appearance of a new enemy inside Zaire, nor did anything in reaction to a mechanized RPA battalion that drove its RG-31s and Toyotas from Camp Ndenzi into Burundi and then entered Zaire through the Gatumba border post, before driving south and disappearing in the direction of Uvira. The Zairian authorities were in total confusion over what was going on and no one investigated.

Unperturbed by reports from the border, Kagame first flew to South Africa, arriving on 18 September 1996 for a series of meetings with top officials. One of his main concerns was to make sure that several large arms contracts would be honoured, no matter what was about to happen in eastern Zaire. Kagame must have returned to Kigali with some sort of guarantee in his pocket. As soon as he was back, on 22 September the RPA artillery opened fire on the FAZ base in Bukavu, intending to pin Zairian troops down while additional Rwandan troops crossed the border.

In early October, with two RPA brigades and infiltrated ADP units in place between Bukavu and Uvira, the Rwandans went into action and assaulted the FAZ base in Lemera. The attackers first infiltrated the village then signalled the start of the attack by dropping a mortar shell on the FAZ barracks, subjecting the same to a simultaneous attack from within, but leaving an escape route for the defenders.

Taken by surprise and shocked by the speed of the attack, the Zairian resistance collapsed and survivors fled into the Fizi region inhabited by the Bembe tribe, where many were killed by the locals in revenge for previous atrocities and looting.

The pattern of the RPA assault on Lemera was to be repeated on a number of occasions in the following days and weeks. Exploiting the heat, humidity and dense vegetation surrounding populous centres, the Rwandans would infiltrate a town that was the target of attack – often in full daylight and disguised as civilians, carrying their weapons in rags, or strapping them onto bicycles – while carefully reconnoitring the area. The infiltrators would then gather at an assigned point ahead of an attack and the defenders would unexpectedly find themselves surrounded, inside and out. Nearly all the objectives taken by the RPA in October, November and December 1996 fell to this tactic and the FAZ was hopelessly incapable of finding any means to counter it.

Offensive on refugee camps

Following the success at Lemera, the RPA paused to reorganize and deploy units into selected positions before continuing, primarily because Kigali needed time to set the political scene for the coming developments. On 17 October, as the establishment of the AFDL was officially announced to the public, what the Zairian authorities described as mysterious armed men but who were actually units of the Rwandan army acting as insurgents, launched their attacks on eleven refugee camps located along the Ruzizi River, that – according to the UNHCR – housed 219,466 people. Although in some of these camps refugees lived alongside ALiR units (for example in Kanganiro), the vast majority were unarmed civilians, and nearly all extremists

Although heavily armed and relatively well supplied, the conglomerate of FAZ units deployed in the Kivus in early 1996 was poorly led and incapable of engaging in serious military operations. *Photo Albert Grandolini Collection*

had left the area before the RPA troops arrived. Nevertheless, on 20 October, after securing the village of Bwegera, the RPA attacked Luvungi, Kanganiro and Rubenga camps. The next day, Lubarika and Luberizi – all vacated, not only by the FAZ but also by the UN-controlled camp security forces – came under attack, followed by Kagunga on 24 October. The same evening, the RPA launched its assault on the town of Uvira. By the following morning, the local FAZ battalion was routed and the Rwandans promptly gathered all the AFDL leaders on site.

The attacks on refugee camps in the Uvira territory caused mass panic and the flight of refugees in several directions. Some left for Fizi and then headed for northern Katanga, others escaped toward the north, many Burundian refugees fled in the direction of Burundi, while others attempted to reach some of the 26 camps in the Bukavu area where the UNHCR estimated there were already around 307,499 refugees.

Advancing from Uvira toward the north, the RPA first reached Nyantende village before splitting into two groups, one continuing on to Bukavu, while the other headed toward the Walungu heartland. On 20 October, they attacked the Kamanyola camp in the Walungu territory, followed by the Nyarubale camp the next day. On 22 October, the huge Kibumba camp, containing around 195,000 refugees, was overrun. RPA troops destroyed a DSP company and decimated a camp security battalion. On 29 October, the Rwandans took Bukavu, the last defenders of which were a group of Burundian FDD insurgents.

The camps in North Kivu where, according to the UNHCR, there were the largest concentrations of Rwandan refugees, including no less than 717,991 people, came under attack on 25 October. Initially the RPA deployed only the infiltrated troops, but with their advance bogging down, heavy artillery firing from inside Rwanda was deployed in addition to mechanized units. During the night of 25/26 October, the RPA attack failed at Katale. FAZ troops, reinforced by camp security forces and a few Hutu extremists, nearly annihilated the attackers, but, in response the Rwandans again opened fire with heavy artillery the following night, causing heavy losses to the defenders. During the same evening four other camps along the Goma–Rutshuru road came under artillery fire from inside Rwanda, eventually causing a massive refugee exodus, mostly toward Goma. The RPA then overran the FAZ base at Rumangabo on 29 October and deployed additional units to cut off all escape routes except the one to the Mugunga camp, where, in the meantime, an uncontrollable mass of at least 500,000 refugees had gathered.

Spontaneous repatriation

The outbreak of violence, reports of heavy fighting and the use of artillery, plus the flight of refugees, caused some international concern, but there was little clarity about the situation in eastern Zaire and, due to the guilt the UN carried as a result of the Rwandan Genocide, the UN seemed loath to intervene. While no one was ready to criticize Kigali, the international community – under UN sanction – began preparing a multinational force (MNF) to enter eastern Zaire and secure the safety of the refugees. The UNHCR in Geneva strongly backed the action, and Canada agreed to lead this force that would enjoy the participation of the USA and western powers, as well as several African nations. The MNF posed a threat to Rwandan plans

US-made M101 105mm howitzer of the same type deployed by the RPA to shell a number of refugee camps inside Zaire in late October 1996. *Photo Creative Commons*

to rid itself of the Hutu threat, and to Kabila's desires to oust Mobutu. The RPA could not pursue the Hutu extremists in the different camps in plain sight of foreign troops. Therefore, not only Rwanda, but also the USA, moved to pre-empt the MNF by publishing reports of the spontaneous repatriation of refugees, while the RPA rushed to complete its operation against the camps. On 1 November 1996, Rwandans opened an attack on Goma from the north and east, again supported by artillery firing from beyond the border (Kigali officially denied any kind of involvement, explaining that the "current conflict ... involves Zairians fighting against Zairians"). FAZ resistance collapsed after only a day of fighting, but not before the retreating troops sated themselves killing and looting.

With Goma – and thus the direct supply line to Rwanda – securely in their pocket, and reinforced by a group of about 60 African-American mercenaries (flown in from the USA via Entebbe to Kigali) deployed from Bukavu to fight the FDD at Mwenga and Kiliba, the RPA consolidated the majority of its units for a large assault on Mugunga and the nearby Lac Vert camp. The attack opened on 8 November, again with an infiltration by the HCU, but the assault was initially held up by an ALiR unit and Mayi-Mayi insurgents from Sake. Following short negotiations, the Mayi-Mayi changed sides, and the Rwandans then entered the hills around the town, thus effectively sealing the camp. The RPA operation culminated with a protracted mortar bombardment of the camp launched on the afternoon of 13 November. The ALiR offered fierce resistance before it was forced to break through the cordon surrounding the camp in the direction of Masasi, taking thousands of refugees with them. Another much smaller group fled in panic toward Walikale. On 15 November, after securing the area, Rwandan troops entered the Mugunga camp and ordered the mass of shocked and completely confused refugees still present to return to Rwanda.

Thus began what Kigali maintains was a spontaneous repatriation. An estimated 600,000 refugees should have returned to Rwanda. However, many observers estimated that only between 350,000 and 500,000 refugees actually crossed the border. Similarly, out of around 77,000 Burundian refugees detained by the RPA attack on Uvira

and herded toward the Burundi border, only 23,000 slowly trickled back across during the following eight months, while around 10,000 managed to make their way to Tanzania. Even taking into account the very uncertain counting methods of refugees and returnees at the borders, this leaves a gap of between 350,000 and 450,000 Rwandan, and between 25,000 and 40,000 Burundian refugees who had disappeared from eastern Zaire by mid-November 1996. What happened to many of them can only be described as another genocide.* During their ever-deepening advance into Zaire between mid-November 1996 and mid-March 1997, the RPA and Banyamulenge militias systematically hunted them down, corralled and killed tens of thousands in cold blood. The full extent of these massacres was not to be understood until much later, when first authoritative reports were published amid much resistance from various western and African officials, but also from the international media.

Gift or curse
One could have expected that from the standpoint of Kigali, once the Hutu refugees were returned to Rwanda, the refugee problem was solved. It was not. Their only victory was that, in reaction to the reports of spontaneous repatriation, the international community quickly dropped the MNF idea and no foreign troops were deployed in eastern Zaire. On the contrary, Rwandan reconnaissance rapidly found that large numbers of refugees had not only survived the repatriation, and massacres, but were fleeing ever deeper into Zaire. They detected one large group west of Masisi and another north of Sake, many people – including several ALiR units – heading west from Bukavu toward Shabunda. Another group was seen, including extremists, running away in the direction of Walikale and small numbers fleeing south around Fizi. Eventually the RPA had to admit that, except for the ALiR unit that had suffered heavy casualties during the fight for Kibumba camp, most of the extremists it was hunting, had managed to escape. The Rwandans thus not only spent plenty of precious time corralling and massacring innocent refugees, but now had to make a decision concerning their next move. Apparently unimpressed, Kigali opted for continuing the hunt and completing the conquest of the Kivus.

Although corseted by the RPA and working under the tight control of the Rwandan military intelligence, the AFDL had to make a similar decision. On 20 November, its leaders met in Goma, originally with the intention of coordinating the establishment of their organization's authority over the Kivus. However, recently returned from Goma – where he managed to stop the RPA troops from removing a large electric generator from the IAP, and in the face of demands for the liberation of all of Zaire – Ngandu began openly

---

* Since it was initially formulated in 1948, in article 2 of the Convention on the Prevention and Punishment of the Crime of Genocide, the definition of the crime has remained substantively the same. It can be found in article 6 of the Rome Statute, which defines the crime of genocide as 'any of the following acts committed with intent to destroy, in whole or in part, a national, ethnical, racial or religious group, as such'. The definition is followed by a series of acts representing serious violations of the right to life and the physical or mental integrity of the members of the group. The Convention also provides that not only the acts themselves are punishable, but also conspiracy to commit genocide, direct and public incitement to commit genocide, the attempt to commit genocide and complicity in genocide. It is the specific intention to destroy an identified group either in whole or in part that distinguishes the crime of genocide from a crime against humanity.

complaining about the heavy control exercised over the AFDL by the Rwandans: the looting of national possessions should be for Zaire's account, not Kigali's. Except for Kabila and few Banyamulenge, most ADFL leaders sided with him, but accepted that their ultimate goal, toppling Mobutu, was impossible without Rwandan support. The insurgents – reinforced to around 6,000 by freely recruiting various members of local militias, defected FAZ troops and the deployment of US mercenaries – continued to follow the RPA advance. Aware

of their lack of training and discipline, their Rwandan commanders primarily deployed them to secure occupied territory and hunt down and massacre fleeing refugees.

Relentless pursuit

The RPA (and AFDL) returned to fighting the FAZ in late November. With three brigades under his command and deployed in eastern Zaire, and with the AFDL boosted to around 5,000 fighters, Kabarebe was able to prepare a large-scale offensive. If measured by the distances his troops had to travel, this was to see the relentless pursuit of the Hutu refugees, who had escaped the early massacres and spontaneous repatriation, deep into North and South Kivu. This operation was three pronged: from Goma and Bukavu toward Butembo and Walikale, from Bukavu toward Shabunda, and from Uvira toward Kalemie in the south. Contrary to initial Rwandan operations, this was to become a less carefully planned and orchestrated operation, and would see the significant involvement of AFDL irregulars. Rwandan reconnaissance regarding targets was nowhere near as precise as those concerning the refugee camps; the terrain was far more rugged and was covered by dense and seemingly endless jungle. Kabarebe and his commanders had to expect resistance from a few minor FAZ units and Hutu extremists, as well as from various other groups, and had to ignore FDD insurgents who were still fighting in South Kivu, on their southern flank. The extent and sustainability of that resistance was actually unknown and in the light of the first intelligence reports of Mobutu's efforts to recruit foreign mercenaries, it was impossible to predict where the RPA might confront what defenders.

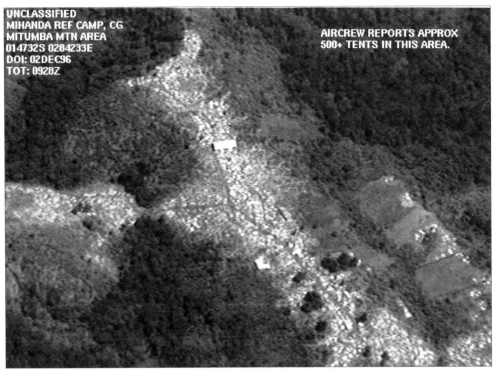

US intelligence was closely tracking the flight of Rwandan refugees deeper into Zaire, following the destruction of camps along the border with Rwanda. This photograph shows a small camp constructed in the Mihanda area near the border between North and South Kivu in December 1996. *Photo US DoD*

This US reconnaissance photograph shows a refugee camp erected near Kilambo, some 45km west of Bukavu, in December 1996. It is almost a certainty that many such photographs and relevant information were supplied to the RPA commanders and played a crucial role in the planning of their subsequent operations. *Photo US DoD*

In summary, the huge expanse of the battlefield, problematic terrain, dense vegetation, poor communications and the complexity of the military operations, practically dictated that the Rwandans could not predict how much and what kind of resupply their units might need and when, as they faced an entirely different set of problems on operational and tactical levels than they had faced in the Kivus. Instead of following a plan developed after months of very careful study, they often had to improvise. The crux of their planning during the following weeks was the availability of a relatively large number of primitive airfields scattered all over Zaire, as well as a few stretches of straight roads. The RPA commanders would search for these on their maps, find them, send their troops to clear and secure the sites and

Laurent Désiré Kabila was installed by Kigali and Kampala as president of the AFDL, here seen in front of the AFDL flag.
Photo Mark Lepko Collection

then bring in supplies with their single BN-2A, several Twin Otters, and Lockheed L-100s (the civilian variant of the C-130 Hercules) of Air Cargo Uganda, as recalled by one of involved pilots:

"We've had two L-100s and were mostly hauling ammunition and supplies between Entebbe and Kigali, sometimes also from various collection points in Eastern Europe. Once Kamina fell, we started flying there as well but the most intensive periods were in August and November 1996."

Meanwhile, and one would assume to the vast relief of the Rwandans, Uganda had decided to join the Rwandan invasion of Zaire. On 15 November 1996, two UPDF battalions crossed the border and launched an advance in the direction of Kasindi – a major rear base of Ugandan insurgents in northeastern Zaire – 10km from the Ugandan border, on the roads to Butembo and Beni (of course Kampala officially denied any kind of involvement or that its troops had indeed crossed the border). The Rwandans met very little resistance in Butembo, which fell on 26 November, while in Beni, the FAZ force of around 1,000 soldiers, reinforced by at least one company of Hutus, detected the approaching RPA battalion of around 500 troops and attempted to intercept them. With the help of infiltrated special troops, the Rwandans recognized this deployment in time and ambushed the FAZ force, routing it in the process. Beni was captured on 3 December.

Meanwhile, the main effort of the offensive developed along the road from Goma in a westerly direction toward Walikale. Behind the RPA, the AFDL insurgents, now increasingly supported by Mayi-Mayi groups, went in pursuit of the refugee survivors, committing additional atrocities in Ngungu, Osso, and especially in the Rukwi area. On the southern prong of this offensive another RPA column advanced from Bukavu toward Shabunda, considered important because of a bridge over the Ulindi River. On 22 November, they captured the Chimanga camp, where the AFDL units murdered a large group of refugees. On 2 December 1996, an RPA unit captured Kamitunga, a gold and diamond centre some 90km west of Bukavu. A week later and farther down the road, the Rwandans reached three makeshift camps around Shabunda, where the UNHCR had registered around 38,000 Hutu refugees. Once again, the FAZ and ALiR beat a hasty retreat while the RPA and AFDL commenced with the slaughter of several thousand civilians, primarily Rwandan

A map showing Rwandan advances into Zaire between October 1996 and March 1997, clearly illustrating the importance of different airfields for the RPA's capability to resupply its troops.

Few details of Ugandan operations in northeastern Zaire in late 1996 are available, but it seems that they were intensively supported by UPDF/AW's Mi-8MTVs, one of which can be seen here deplaning a troop of soldiers who are wearing an interesting mix of uniforms and equipment.
Photo Mark Lepko Collection

One of two L-100s operated by Uganda Air Cargo (or Air Cargo Uganda) during the late 1990s was this aircraft, registered as 5X-UCF.
Photo Melting Tarmac Images

Hutu refugees, but also any Zairians who attempted to help them or collaborated with international NGOs and UN organizations. By mid-March 1997, these camps had been duly 'cleansed'.

Because of the necessity to mop up refugees remaining in the Kivus, the political manoeuvring that was necessary in order to secure the cover-up of Rwandan involvement in Zaire to prevent the deployment of an MNF, and the supply problems caused by the poor road networks and availability of very few airstrips, the next phase of the RPA–AFDL advance was to develop very slowly. On 7 December a combined RPA–AFDL column reached the village of Hombo on the border between North and South Kivu. There they split into several groups: the RPA contingent continued to advance in the direction of Walikale, while the AFDL stayed in the area to hunt

down the refugees and hold public meetings for the attention of the Zairian people, during which they accused Hutu refugees of being collectively responsible for the genocide of the Tutsis in Rwanda, and were running away because they were all guilty. The insurgents also claimed that the pigs – as they called the Hutu refugees – were planning to commit genocide against Zairian civilians in the region.

The Rwandans reached Walikale on 16 December where they spent two days fighting scattered FAZ and Hutu units. North of the town, an RPA battalion swiftly infiltrated and overpowered a small ex-FAR unit in the Kariki refugee camp, disarmed its troops and executed them. The next wave of RPA units bypassed north of Walikale, leaving the area to the AFDL before continuing their advance to the North/South Kivu border and Maniema Province.

Testing times

Once the possibility of the UN deploying peacekeeping troops in eastern Zaire was definitely averted, there was some bickering in Kigali, Bukavu and Goma about future operations. Reportedly, upon occupying all of North and South Kivu – an area four times the size of Rwanda – Kagame was still only interested in establishing a buffer zone, and thus preferred to halt the advance. Kabarebe and his aides were in high spirits and advocated a continuation of the hunt for Hutus. They knew that the core of the ALiR had reached Tingi-Tingi, a village with an airstrip west of the Osso River, where four makeshift camps with 120,000 Hutu refugees had been identified. The camps were almost exclusively filled with civilians turned away by FAZ troops deployed for the protection of Kisangani. However, another camp near the village of Amisi, 70km east of that site, contained around 40,000 Rwandan Hutus, including an substantial ALiR cadre (and their families) who were using the Tingi-Tingi

Walikale was one of the aims of the second Rwandan offensive into Zaire launched in November 1996. This area was not only important because thousands of Hutu refugees had fled there, but also because it included one of few airfields (actually a stretch of tar road) with a hardened runway in this part of the country, enabling operations of heavier transport aircraft. *Photo Guido Potters*

Rugged terrain, dense jungle and a lack of good roads in the Kivus considerably slowed the Rwandan advance in early December 1996. The solution the RPA found was to capture local airfields and intensively deploy chartered 'civilian' transport aircraft, primarily those operated by companies run by Victor Bout. Here is seen a typical bush village in South Kivu. *Photo Guido Potters*

camps as a recruitment and training facility with a view to joining the announced FAZ counteroffensive into the Kivus. With the nearest RPA units only a few days' march away and the FAZ fleeing at the sight of them, the commander of the RPA operations in Zaire insisted on continuing the advance. The leaders of the AFDL liked the idea. Controlling the entire area from Beni in the north to Uvira in the south was all well and good but an advance in a westerly direction was far more promising with regard to their objectives, which were centred on toppling Mobutu.

Kigali eventually decided to do two things. The first was to launch an operation outside the Kivus, with the intention of testing reactions from Kinshasa, as well as those of its allies. A suitable target was found at Bunia, 400km due north of Goma, where the FAZ had concentrated several units, primarily a battalion of the Civil Guard, perhaps a company of the 31st Parachute Brigade, at least one company of ALiR fighters and a battalion of regular UNITA insurgents from Angola, led by Angolan General Abilio Kamalata (nicknamed 'Numa'). The force under Kamalata's control was well entrenched, but his unit had been weakened while deploying in Zaire: trucked all the way from Kamina to Bunia, it suffered losses while underway to the battlefield with many of its soldiers vanishing into the jungle. The RPA reached the area in mid-December 1996, followed by one Ugandan battalion and a small AFDL unit. As usual, the Rwandans

infiltrated the town before assaulting it on 20 December, but their attack was checked by UNITA and Zairian paratroopers. Then the Zairian defence collapsed, reportedly because the paratroopers ran out of ammunition, but in fact, because most of them defected. The UNITA veterans offered stiff resistance but were overrun after 12 hours and General Kamalata barely managed to escape with a few survivors. Bunia fell on 24 December and the Ugandans then swiftly captured the gold mines of Kilo Moto.

The second issue Kigali had to tackle was that of the AFDL military leader Ngandu. This Zairian patriot was already at odds with Kabarebe and other Rwandan commanders because he opposed their campaign of looting. Thus Kigali decided to get rid of him. When the first uprising of the Mayi-Mayi against the Rwandans erupted in the Butembo area in late December 1996, the RPA requested that Ngandu take care of this issue. While underway to Butembo, Ngandu's bodyguards were removed and replaced by Rwandans who usually protected Kabila. Careless enough to accept this and go anyway, Ngandu was, after early January 1997, never seen again.

Considering what was meanwhile going on in Kinshasa, the period between mid-December 1996 and mid-January 1997, during which the Rwandans practically halted their advance, could have proved a fatal mistake: namely, Kigali's preoccupation with destroying the remaining Hutus in the Kivus and capturing Bunia offered the

The runway at Walikale, typical of around 50 different landing sites used by aircraft deployed to support the RPA's advance into Zaire in late 1996 and early 1997. *Photo Guido Potters*

This An-8, last seen at Sharjah IAP in 2000, was operated by Victor Bout's AirCess in Rwanda in the late 1990s, registered as EL-WHL. It was frequently sighted not only at Kigali IAP, but also in Goma and around other places in eastern Zaire. *Photo Richard Vandervord*

Kivus – including two weak artillery battalions (totalling only 12 guns), a battalion of the DSP and another company of the SARM – while appointing two DSP generals as governors to Goma and Bukavu. Their deployment was very slow and most units only arrived during the second half of November. And indeed, the two artillery battalions were soon overrun by the advancing Rwandans, losing all their equipment in the process. Not identifying themselves with the local population, and even less so with the thousands of refugees, the other FAZ units rapidly turned around and withdrew toward Kisangani and Kindu.

Without knowledge of the US support for Rwandan operations, and confused by contradictory statements of US officials in Kigali and Washington (who denied any kind of Rwandan involvement or US ties to the AFDL), and Kinshasa (who denounced the uprising as a Rwandan and Ugandan invasion), even Paris needed several weeks to find out what exactly was going on. This is not to say that French intelligence was not already in place; as far as is known, a DC-8 Sarique ELINT gatherer had operated over eastern Zaire on a number of occasions through 1996, probably in an attempt to intercept radio transmissions by the AFDL and the RPA. In this fashion, the French learned of the presence of US advisers, primarily PMC operators, and of Rwandan and latterly Ugandan involvement.

However, they neither interpreted this as an operation supported by Washington, nor as a full-scale Rwandan invasion. Unsurprisingly, Paris never decided to intervene militarily. Instead, it left Mobutu to deal with specific circles within the French intelligence and military apparatus, to attempt to save the Zairian government in a fashion that had historically proved successful: recruitment of foreign mercenaries.

With hindsight, it is easy to blame Mobutu and his aides, as well as the French, for being naïve enough to believe that any kind of mercenary action could change the situation on the battlefields of eastern Zaire. However, it cannot be stressed enough, that like everyone else – except the leadership of the RPA and the AFDL, and certain circles in the USA – no one knew what was really going on there.

Terminally ill with prostate cancer, Mobutu was not only unwilling, but unable, to make crucial political decisions. In September and October 1996 he was undergoing treatment in Europe. More than any kind of insurgency in eastern Zaire he feared a military coup, or at least a power struggle at top military and political level, that would neutralize the remnants of his power. Except for very few family members, he was suspicious of nearly all his military leaders and continued reshuffling them. By 1995, General Mahele had been replaced by Eluki Monga Aundu as army chief of staff. Aundu was

government of Zaire a breathing space in which to reorganize the FAZ and launch a counteroffensive against the Rwandans.

Legion Blanc

It is quite obvious that Mobutu and his top military commanders never realized what was actually going on in eastern Zaire during the latter part of 1996. For example, due to the poor state of the entire country, especially communications, it took three days for news of the fall of Goma to reach Kinshasa. There, the reports caused not a little amusement. Only General Mahele advocated an immediate deployment of FAZ reinforcements to the east. Even after the collapse of FAZ units in the Kivus, the Zairian generals were extremely slow to react and it took their French advisers much convincing to galvanize them into action – which resulted in next to nothing.

The first reaction in Kinshasa was to send reinforcements to the

This DC-8 Sarique ELINT/SIGINT-gathering reconnaissance aircraft of the French Air Force operated on several occasions over eastern Zaire in 1996. *Photo Jean-Francois Lipka*

Still from a BBC documentary showing the cockpit of the sole SOKO NJ-21 Jastreb two-seater conversion trainer and light striker sold to Zaire, on the apron of Gbadolite airfield. The aircraft was operated by a group of Serbian pilots and ground personnel in early 1997. *Photo Pit Weinert Collection*

fired in early November 1996 after the débâcle in the Kivus and was replaced by General Kpana Baramoto, who had to be released from house arrest for this purpose. Baramoto's tenure did not last very long either. After Mobutu's return to Kinshasa on 17 December 1996, Baramoto was replaced by Mahele. While this reshuffling prevented any of these officers from establishing themselves in power, it also prevented them from bringing the military under control and launching a counteroffensive too.

Under pressure from the French, Mobutu next stuck a deal with his government, several wealthy businessmen and representatives from French political and military circles to finance a foreign mercenary force. What the Zairian president had in his mind was the likes of a mercenary action that helped establish him in power in the mid-1960s. Out of touch with reality, Mobutu did not know that those days were long gone; worse yet, he ordered this effort to be undertaken in a multi-pronged fashion, partially via the ministry of defence and partially via his personal aides, thus further increasing the split within different cliques of the FAZ.

Amazingly, although Mobutu and his generals, as well as friendly businessmen, had access to vast personal wealth and could easily have paid for foreign military contractors and new equipment, they were not willing to do so. Concerned about a possible collapse of the government, they preferred to pocket as much as possible and quarrelled over the distribution of funds, instead of paying foreigners to keep them in power.

The ministry of defence selected a retired Belgian colonel, Christian Tavernier, to recruit a force that would protect the city of Kisangani. Tavernier had been close to Mobutu since the mid-1960s when he served as commander of the 14 Commando ANC and later ran a company specializing in military provisioning, training and consulting, with strong links to French intelligence circles. He had recent experience in eastern Zaire, where he had advised former FAR officers in the organization of the ALiR, and thus had a relatively good picture of the situation. Convinced there was enough time and, in an attempt to defuse tensions with Rwanda, he decided to collect and relocate the Hutus to Kamina in southern Zaire. In the meantime, he wanted to reorganize the FAZ and retrain it with the help of foreigners.

Keeping in mind the limited amount of funding he was likely to receive for his services, Tavernier was left with little choice but to save wherever he could. He recruited a small group of around 30 western

mercenaries, primarily French and Belgian, but also a Portuguese, a Chilean and an Italian. They signed renewable three-month contracts at a monthly remuneration of around US$5,000. The majority of the rest of his force consisted of Serbs with fresh combat experience from the various conflicts in the former Yugoslavia, who proved cheaper due to the poor economic situation in their own country. During a meeting at Hotel Turist in Belgrade, in late December 1996, Tavernier's agents managed to recruit 276 men. These included a few active and retired officers of the former Yugoslav army and air force, led by an officer from Kosovo, known as Colonel Dominic Yugo, and 80 Bosnian Serbs, members of various local militias, led by Lieutenant Milorad 'Misa' Palemis. The pay for this group was not as good, though a few of their leaders pocketed as much as US$20,000 a month, with the average mercenary only getting US$1,000 a month. Half was paid in advance, but the balance – which was due on arrival in Zaire – was rarely ever paid.

Tavernier's plan for their deployment basically remained the same as originally intended. Upon arriving in Kinshasa by commercial flight, the French-speaking mercenaries were deployed via Kisangani to Watsa by a chartered Russian Antonov transport. Once in the field, they split into Team Alpha, led by a Frenchman named Charles, and Team Bravo, led by a Belgian, and were rushed to the battlefield in an attempt to curb the Rwandan-led advance. This contingent was supported by one BAE Andover medium transport, a single Pilatus PC-6B Turbo Porter light transport and liaison aircraft, with four Mi-24 helicopter gunships acquired from the Ukraine – with armament, ammunition and the necessary pilots and ground crews.*

The deployment of the Serbian contingent took slightly longer because their task was more complex. They were to secure the airfields of Kisangani and Gbadolite, provide aerial support for French-speaking mercenaries and train DSP troops in the use of weapons ordered from Serbia. The Serbian contingent was to be heavily armed. To equip them, Tavernier purchased five MiG-21PFMs fighter-bombers and one MiG-21UM two-seater conversion trainer, two Antonov An-26 medium transports and four SOKO J-21 Jastreb light strikers

---

* A TV documentary made by the BBC team that visited Gbadolite in early 1997 showed a single CASA C.212 light transport. It remains unknown whether any such aircraft was directly involved in supporting operations of the Legion Blanc.

from Serbia.* Furthermore, he ordered a large stock of Serbian-made weapons, including locally manufactured AK-47 replicas (designated M-70B1s), M53 machine guns, M57 grenade launchers, RPG-7s, 60mm mortars, LAW anti-tank weapons, SA-7s, MANPADs and plenty of anti-personnel mines. This armament, including related ammunition and communication equipment, was delivered to Kisangani in at least eight flights of chartered Ilyushin Il-76 transports during the first half of January 1997. They were followed by two massive Antonov An-124 transports that delivered around 200 tons of ammunition, purchased from Belarus, on 12 January.

Thus came into being the Legion Blanc or White Legion, the establishment of which encouraged the Zairian prime minister, Leon Kengo wa Dondo, to boast about "a total and crushing offensive, which will spare no enemy, Zairian or foreign" before the mercenaries and their equipment arrived in Zaire on 2 January 1997.

Mobutu's keystone cops

Starting in late November 1996, the FAZ began massing its forces southeast of Kisangani and in Kindu, with the intention of launching a counteroffensive into the Kivus. Centred around the remnants of the 31st Airborne Brigade and two battalions of the 41st Commando Brigade, survivors of the Civil Guard – who withdrew from Bunia and looted each village they passed through – were corseted by companies of the SARM and supported by a weak artillery battalion, one of the FAZA's DHC-5 Caribous and the last few Puma and Alouette helicopters. The Zairian forces were put under the direct command of General Mahele. This concentration and its commander were a clear sign of desperation. Mahele repeatedly proved to be the most capable of Mobutu's generals, a competent commander (by FAZ standards) and popular with the troops. But he was not a member of the president's Ngandi tribe and was very unpopular among various cliques of the FAZ officer corps. Many of his subordinates refused outright to listen to him and he never managed to establish a unified command over this force.

Without sufficient forces to maintain a continuous front line, and lacking useful intelligence on the origins, intentions and capabilities of his opponents, Mahele deployed his troops in three sectors. In the north was Sector N, where major strongpoints were established to protect bridges on the Osso and Lubilinga rivers, close to the border between North Kivu and the Maniema Province. Sector C covered Kindu, and Sector S Kalemie. During January 1997, these positions were strengthened by foreign mercenaries. Teams Alpha and Bravo were deployed at Watsa to train the local FAZ units. A UNITA regiment was deployed at Bafwasende, the ALiR survivors from Walikale and their new recruits from Tingi-Tingi were concentrated at Amisi, together with at least a battalion of FAZ troops. Kindu was protected by one battalion of the FAZ, the remnants of the FDD and Bembe militia.

To the rear of this FAZ force Colonel Tavernier set up the Legion

Blanc HQ in Kisangani, where his Serbian mercenaries attempted to train Zairian SARM troops on weapons that had arrived with them, while heavily mining and fortifying the approaches. However, Tavernier soon found himself facing impossible odds. Communication

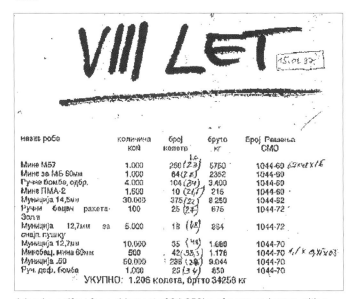

A copy of a fax sent from a Serbian representative to a French official involved in recruiting, organizing and arming the Legion Blanc, this discusses the details of a shipment of 115,535kg of arms with the help of Occidental Airlines aircraft from Yugoslavia to Zaire in mid-January 1997.

A load manifest for a shipment of 34,258kg of arms and ammunition dispatched on 15 January 1997 from Belgrade to Kinshasa. VIII Let stands for 8th Flight, meaning this is the eighth shipment of this kind. The arms in question include 1,000 M57 anti-tank mines, 1,500 PMA-2 anti-personnel mines, 4,000 hand grenades, 60mm mortars, 100 Zolja launchers for anti-tank rockets and quantities of various ammunition.

---

* The two An-26s are known to have been serialled 71351 and 71352 while serving with the former Yugoslav Air Force. Two of the J-21s are known to have been the former Yugoslav Air Force serials 24151 (c/n 057, which became FG-483 in Zaire), and 24422 (c/n 022, which became FG-482). However, nothing is known about the background of the MiG-21s, and alternative reports indicate they actually arrived in Zaire from North Korea via China, together with a consignment of 600 tons of arms and ammunition. See Associated Press and *Boston Globe* reports from 8–10 April 1997.

with the Serbian contingent proved extremely problematic, very few spoke English or French, and none had any command of Swahili or any other local language. They refused to listen to anybody but their superiors – especially the brutal Colonel Yugo – who operated at their own discretion but had no useful maps. Within a few days after arriving in the Kisangani area, most were sick with dysentery and malaria, while many spent their days getting drunk and harassing civilians. While the original Zairian expectations had been such that they had dubbed the Serbs 'the specialists of warfare', loud of mouth but abysmally short on courage, the Serbs proved nearly useless and were disparaged by the locals as *ces cochons-la* (the bastards).

The promised mercenary air force didn't fare much better. Flown by a US pilot who called himself Roland, the sole Andover proved useful in ferrying men and cargo between Kinshasa and Kisangani (it probably survived the war; it was last seen at an airfield in Kisangani in March 1997), while at least one of the two An-26s sold to Zaire by Serbia was abandoned intact at N'Djili IAP. The much lighter Turbo Porter is known to have been lost when it was flown into a ten-metre-high anthill and crashed a few days after its arrival in Zaire.

Meanwhile, the Serbian technicians assembled their Jastrebs and prepared them for combat, which proved anything but easy, considering an acute shortage of fuel. Another problem was the same issue experienced by most of the Serbian mercenaries: they had a massive problem with liquor. One of the Serbian pilots, Colonel Turcinovic (ret.) crashed his J-21 Jastreb while making a foolish ultra-

low-level pass over the town of Gbadolite and clipping a lamppost with a wing, only a few days after arriving in Zaire; the plane crashed directly into a café full of FAZ troops and foreigners, killing at least ten. Reportedly, Turcinovic was nursing a hangover from the night before.[*]

Despite many other problems, primarily related to the lack of fuel, the remaining three former Serbian aircraft were subsequently redeployed to Kisangani and then to Kindu, followed by Mi-24s. The Serbian pilots flew their first combat sorties against Shabunda and Walikale in early February 1997, reportedly flying so high that their bombs missed by several kilometres. On 17 February, they flew their longest-ranged mission, taking off from Kindu to hit Bukavu. Flown under direct order from the Zairian minister of defence, Genersl Likulia Bolongo – bypassing Mahele – the attack on Bukavu occurred around 16h00, bombing the marketplace and densely populated areas in the centre of the town, where 19 civilians were killed and between 37 and 50 wounded.[†] Bolongo later maintained that the strike hit only military targets "in surgical fashion".

The Ukrainians delivered and assembled their four Mi-24s and deployed them to Kindu, but these flew only very sporadically. The FAZA repeatedly failed to respond to their calls for resupply of ammunition and fuel. Furthermore, one Mi-24 (probably that coded 9T-HM4) crashed, killing the crew of four on 27 March 1997, and another (9T-HM3) developed technical difficulties (rotor vibrations) and was seldom flown.

The far more capable MiG-21s – even though completely unsuitable for Zairian conditions – never became operational. They arrived at Gbadolite during March or April 1997 and were only partially assembled before the end of the war. Therefore, the much-promised Serbian top cover for the FAZ and foreign mercenaries never really materialized.

Meanwhile, midway through the arrival of the Legion Blanc, and thus much too early, the strongmen in Kinshasa had started pushing Mahele into a counteroffensive, and he acted accordingly. In late January 1997 he ordered a 500–700-strong battalion to advance from Kisangani on Bafwasende in the north and on Walikale in the south, and from Kindu on Bukavu, and from Kalemie toward Uvira. They were to be supported by several artillery battalions, but primarily through Ukrainian-flown Mi-24s and Serbian-flown Jastrebs, based in Kindu.

Battle for Maniema

Kabarebe faced no such problems. Through mid-January he reorganized his forces into three major groups, each centred around one reinforced RPA battalion. The northern group was advancing through Haut Zaire in the direction of Isiro, with Ugandans supporting their right flank, advancing on Watsa and then Aru. The central group was to approach Kisangani along two different axes: along the road from Walikale via Bafwasende (northern route) and

Above: FAZ troops waiting for the landing of an FAZA SA 330C Puma helicopter somewhere in the bush. A soldier armed with a Belgian FN Minimi can be seen in the foreground. Although theoretically well-enough equipped and trained to halt the Rwandan and AFDL advance, the Zairian military usually proved completely hopeless. *Photo Albert Grandolini Collection*

Despite his best efforts, General Donat Lieko Mahele, Mobutu's most capable military leader, proved unable to organize not only an FAZ counteroffensive into the Kivus, but also the defence of Maniema Province and Kisangani. *Photo Mark Lepko Collection*

---

[*] Legend has it that a group of Turcinovic's colleagues left the café demolished by the Jastreb wreckage of minutes before the crash, supposedly because they found the local beer prices too high.

[†] 'Zairian Military Jets Bomb Civilians in Rebel-Held Town', The *New York Times*, 18 February 1997; 'Zaire: Defence Ministry Says Air Force to Intensify Bombing Raids', *Vox du Zaire*, Kinshasa, 18 February 1997; & Ngbanda, p. 203.

FAZ troops deploying along bush roads east of Kisangani, January 1997. *Photo Albert Grandolini Collection*

from Walikale via Lubutu (southern route). The southern RPA brigade advanced from Uvira toward Fizi and Kalemie.

The inevitable multiple clashes that followed within days resulted in the most bitter battles of the war. Between 19 and 20 January, the RPA troops, reinforced by a contingent of US mercenaries, and advancing from Walikale to Lubutu, clashed with an FAZ column that had reached the easternmost bridge on the Oso River, near Nia Nia and in the village of Mungele. What exactly happened there remains unknown. What is certain is that both sides suffered casualties and what was left of the Zairian battalion subsequently fled the battlefield in the direction of Lubutu. Reportedly, the Rwandans even lost several of their US mercenaries (the bodies of two should have been returned by the French authorities and a third is said to have been buried in situ). Little is known about what exactly happened with the Angolans in Bafwasende either, as when the Rwandans reached that town they found it undefended.

What is definitely clear is that the RPA subsequently accelerated its advance, capturing the Amisi camp amid an intense running battle in which it would have suffered additional losses. The ALiR struggled to buy time for most of the camp's population to escape and resettle in the Tingi-Tingi camps on 7 February, but this was of little significance because, once unleashed, Kabarebe would not stop his dash for refugee camps, no matter how deep into Zaire the Hutus were withdrawing. Two days later, the RPA reached the village of Mukwanyama, 18km from Tingi-Tingi, prompting the final battle with the ALiR in the course of this war. The Hutus experienced such a defeat that their resistance completely collapsed. Scattering in all directions, most of their leaders fled to Nairobi in Kenya on board an Antonov transport chartered from Victor Bout. On the morning of 1

March, the RPA entered the Tingi-Tingi camp and indiscriminately killed all its remaining occupants, mostly the sick and wounded being treated in the dispensary, and unaccompanied minors.

If this major prong of the FAZ counteroffensive thus collapsed before managing to launch an attack, that in the Central Sector – the advance from Kindu toward Bukavu – never even materialized, while the southernmost prong, launched out of Kalemie, faltered within two days of its commencement. The reasons for the failure of the FAZ to launch an advance from Kindu relate primarily to the lack of trained crews for the few heavy weapons that were available. Apparently the local FAZ commanders found that they only had one operational mortar crew and not a single operator trained on the BM-21 multiple-rocket launchers.

Nevertheless, the FAZ and the Bembe militia subsequently put up stiff resistance when the RPA advanced on Fizi. They blew up nearly half the bridges south of Uvira, considerably slowing the Rwandan advance and several times ambushed columns approaching villages, forcing the RPA to respond with all its firepower, in turn causing heavy destruction and even more casualties among local civilians. Broken remnants of around 200 soldiers of an FAZ battalion, composed of Babembe troops, were eventually forced to withdraw to Burundi, and, on 3 February, the RPA took the port of Kalemie. When RPA intelligence discovered that not a single intact Zairian army unit was left west of Lake Tanganyika, it ordered a rapid advance toward the Congo River. On 23 February, the Rwandans reached Kalima and four days later entered the town of Kindu – by then completely deserted by the FAZ – massacring hundreds of refugees who had managed to escape from the Shabunda area.

Even less is known about what happened when the Rwandans

Lost in the jungle. What exactly happened to specific FAZ units deployed to counter the RPA advance on Kisangani remains unknown. While at least some of them initially offered serious resistance, eventually all fell apart or fled the Kisangani battlefield in the direction of Lubutu.
Photo Albert Grandolini Collection

reached Watsa to clash with the French and Belgians, and the FAZ troops they had trained. Available reports indicate that Ugandan troops captured Mahagi, cutting off the only land supply route.* The mercenaries put up stiff resistance, employing machine-gun teams, snipers and light mortars to inflict heavy casualties on the attackers – before the sole Andover transport used to support them was hit by ground fire. This is the most likely reason for the ultimate collapse of their defence. Colonel Tavernier subsequently complained bitterly about the lack of resupply.† Whatever happened, teams Alpha and

Bravo fell back toward Kisangani and the FAZ troops were routed at Watsa on 25 January, after which, the Rwandans and Ugandans advanced on Isiro, securing it on 10 February.‡

Fall of Kisangani
The failure of the FAZ counteroffensive in January and the continuous rebel advance in February 1997 completely demoralized the Zairian military and its foreign mercenaries. The mighty FAZ proved spectacularly ineffective, while the foreigners proved to be too little and too late to improve the situation and morale. Not keen to fight for the Zairians on their own, let down by lack of supplies and complaining about not being paid, the Serbs also withdrew to Kisangani and were subsequently sent home, followed by the French, Belgian and other mercenaries.

Nevertheless, the RPA approached Kisangani in a very cautious fashion, probing local FAZ positions while searching for remaining concentrations of Hutu refugees and cutting off all land connections to the city. Following recent experiences from the Maniema Province, and considering reports about the presence of strong Zairian army contingents and foreign mercenaries, Kabarebe (appointed RPA chief of operations around this time) and his commanders obviously expected fierce resistance and therefore concentrated two battalions and a strong AFDL force – a total of some 6,000 troops supported by mortars and artillery – for their attack on Kisangani.

---

* An earlier version of the battle between Franco-Belgian mercenaries and rebels, provided to the author by a source who prefers to remain anonymous, describes a major clash that occurred at the Nzoro Bridge. According to the source, a force of some 20,000 rebels was pitted against the mercenaries, who returned fire with snipers and 60mm mortars only, supposedly causing immense losses. Along the same variant of "the rebels kept coming", Tavernier's group was forced to accept the futility of its effort and fall back toward Kisangani, where their stories about "masses of rebels" would then have discouraged the Serbs. However, subsequent research did not reveal a trace of evidence of a combined RPA-AFDL force totalling 20,000 fighters at any time during the First Congo War. It is also certain that none of its three major task forces that advanced through the western Kivus in January 1997 totalled more than around 2,000 fighters and that none of these suffered anything like the losses described by the source in question. From descriptions of the tactics usually employed by the RPA, it is completely out of character that the Rwandans and the AFDL insurgents would attempt any kind of frontal assault.

† 'Advisers Say FAZ in a Tangle', Radio Brussels via FBIS, 23 February 1997. Specifically, Tavernier explained that the FAZ was in a bad position, that his forces fought "well-organized armed units coming from Uganda", that these forces were very effective, carrying out well-conceived attacks on government positions, and that the balance was "running against us … it is an unfortunate situation with almost no logistics".

‡ It was in Wamba, 100km south of Isiro, that the qualitative and quantitative weakness of the FAZ became obvious, when the town was taken by three insurgents on a motorbike, with one carrying a lance, another a knife and the third a pistol.

However, the FAZ forces in front of them were already in the process of disintegration, capable only of herding thousands of Hutu refugees toward Ubundu. The Rwandans approached the area on 6 March 1997 and first overpowered a small ex-FAR unit that defended a makeshift refugee camp at Njale. This caused such a panic among the refugees that several hundred drowned while trying to cross the Lubilinga River. Many others were subsequently massacred. The last intact ALiR brigade, estimated at some 1,000 fighters, managed to pass the Lubutu–Kisangani road before this was blocked by the RPA, and settled into two makeshift camps between Lubyoa and Maiko, on the right bank of the Congo River on 12 March, where they were resupplied with weapons and ammunition by DSP troops. Led through the jungle around Kisangani by one of the locals, the Rwandans reached these camps two days later. Infiltrating them, they swiftly overcame the defence and captured at least 470 uniformed Hutus, all of whom were summarily executed. Something similar almost happened to the main group of the Serbian mercenary contingent. According to official Kigali reports, they "were trying to fight a conventional war against our guerrilla operation" and were defeated by being outflanked, which forced survivors to flee through the Garamba forest all the way to Sudan.

In Kisangani, the reinforced 48th (Independent) Battalion FAZ was under the command of General Numbi Kaleme, closely supervised by General Lobima Amela (FAZ chief of staff) and General Mabilo Mulimbi (CO Kisangani military region). Before the battle, Kaleme gave his troops one last speech, haranguing them with patriotism, the need to defend the country and their homes, and cautioning them of reprisals if they did not fight. Then Kaleme ordered them to advance on Bafwasende, some 60km northeast of Kisangani, where they ambushed one of the advancing RPA-AFDL columns on 10 March, forcing the enemy to stop their advance for several days. However, their effort was in vain when scores of troops defected while the Rwandans were still approaching, and even more followed as soon as they heard the sound of gunfire. When Kaleme continued insisting on resistance, a mutiny broke out, with some soldiers defecting to the rebel side. Completely demoralized, the rest of the FAZ collapsed and ran toward Isangi, looting, killing and raping as they went. Those Serbian mercenaries still in the city fled aboard their helicopters after blowing up their HQ.* Evacuated to Gbadolite, they were subsequently all flown back to Belgrade. Tavernier, after being denied overall command of the FAZ and mercenary troops in the Kisigani area, reportedly found himself detained by Zairian authorities for "failing to defend the eastern cities" and for "betrayal".

Kisangani thus fell after relatively little fighting on 15 March 1997, but not without the FAZA losing its last operational SA 330 Puma helicopter. This was left behind at Simisini airport because one of its engines malfunctioned and was subsequently burned. The Rwandans captured both local airports intact and immediately launched an air bridge to bring in supplies and ammunition.

Angolan intervention

On the Rwandan side, the situation could not have been better. Although their small and relatively weak units operated independently of each other, separated by hundreds of kilometres of dense jungle

---

* The last of the Serbian mercenaries, including a number of wounded, were evacuated to Belgrade on a Ukrainian aircraft on 6 April 1997.

and rugged terrain, and in cooperation with flimsy groups of AFDL insurgents in their rear, the Zairian resistance all but ended with the fall of Kisangani. Much of the local population greeted the RPA and AFDL troops as liberators, leaving them free to stage search operations in and around the city and massacre additional refugees. Some 80,000 Hutu civilians were still in the area and most of them gathered in three makeshift camps between Kisangani and the town of Ubundu. The Rwandans and insurgents barred any aid from reaching them and encouraged the local population to attack not only the refugees, but also anyone who attempted to help them. Through April 1997 between 60 and 120 refugees in the camps outside Kisangani were dying each day from disease, malnutrition and exhaustion. On 22 April, the RPA troops securing Kigali IAP were redeployed to two of these camps, and theatrically murdered more than 200 civilians in the presence of several senior Rwandan officers.

In regards to their military position, Kabarebe and his troops were now in a much better situation. With Kisangani and its two airports in their hands, the supply situation of the RPA and the AFDL improved considerably, being rapidly resupplied with help from Victor Bout's aircraft. Furthermore, they were soon to receive significant – and most welcome – reinforcements in form of combat-hardened veteran mechanized troops. In early January 1997, two key Angolan officials, national security adviser, General Helder Vier Dias, and secretary-general of the ruling party in Angola, the MPLA, Lopo do Nascimiento, arrived in Bukavu. Their intention was to gather intelligence about the situation on the ground and seek additional information regarding the AFDL's and the RPA/ADFL alliance's standpoint regarding UNITA and Angola. As soon as Dias and do Nascimiento realized that the Rwandans, Ugandans and the insurgents were at war with UNITA, they returned to Luanda to recommend an Angolan intervention. Between 12 and 25 February, Il-76 and An-12 transports of the Angolan Air Force flew the entire 24 Mechanized Regiment of the Angolan army and two battalions of the FNLC to Kigali and Bukavu. This contingent would reach the battlefield in mid-March 1997.

The drive-through war

The fall of Kisangani had far-reaching consequences. Whatever was left of the image of the FAZ as a military organization, or the morale of its remaining troops, was now completely demolished. Worse yet – from the Zairian standpoint – was that the government had managed to alienate much of the army through the recruitment of foreign mercenaries. While these received far better pay (and most of them indeed got paid), they still proved ineffective in combat, although ostensibly superior to Zairian soldiers. Unsurprisingly, as the frustrated survivors of FAZ units in Kisangani fled west, they dissolved into bands, looted civilian properties and public buildings, including hospitals, health centres, schools and places of worship. In the northern Ubangi district, in the Equateur Province, disgruntled DSP soldiers even looted the residences of former dignitaries of the Mobutu government. Whatever the FAZ troops failed to take with them was taken by RPA troops following closely on their heels.

On the other side, the confidence of the Rwandans and the AFDL grew tremendously, and the image of the insurgents improved dramatically. Until capturing Kisangani, many saw the war as simply another insurgency in eastern Zaire. Better-informed observers might have seen it as a Rwandan gambit to create a buffer zone along

Around 100 flights of An-12 (seen here) and Il-76 transports of the Angolan Air Force were required to deploy the entire 24 Mechanized Regiment of the FAA, its vehicles, equipment and ammunition to Kigali and Bukavu in early March 1997. *Photo Chris Mak*

Aircraft of various of companies belonging to Victor Bout and his local associates were instrumental in the rapid redeployment of RPA troops into central and southern Zaire in April/May 1997. Although often very old, sometimes even flown without the necessary operational permissions, they provided a highly valuable service. This An-12, registration ER-ACK, was operated by Ugandan KM Airlines between 1997 and 2000, and was almost certainly used to haul supplies for advancing Rwandan and Ugandan militaries. *Photo Michael Fabry*

the border with Zaire, with Kabila a mere frontman for foreign interests. After Kisangani, popular support for the AFDL – and its recruitment – soared. All of a sudden, toppling Mobutu was no longer a pipedream, but a near certainty.

Indeed, Mobutu was in such a heightened state of panic that he made another crucial mistake: he ordered nearly the entire DSP (less two battalions) to be redeployed to protect Gbadolite, his native town, leaving General Mahele with only 2,500 FAZ troops and various security contingents of the SARM and SNIP in Kinshasa. Although not showing any signs of stepping down, Mobutu eventually agreed to enter negotiations with Kabila, and offer him and AFDL representatives several seats in government. The insurgents, however, took part in these talks more as a means of receiving publicity than with any serious intention of joining Mobutu's government. Subsequently, the RPA/AFDL advance accelerated at a pace. Since the FAZ now posed no threat and offered no resistance, the war turned into a race.

Next, the Rwandans and insurgents turned south. Moving large contingents to various airfields and airstrips in central Zaire, they rushed in the direction of the crucial Katanga Province, the mineral resources capital. The local population began to welcome the advancing RPA and AFDL troops with open arms. When less than 300 Rwandan soldiers and insurgents approached the outskirts of Lubumbashi in a pincer movement (partially through northwestern Zambia) in early April 1997, the entire FAZ 21st Brigade (around 2,500 strong) raised a white flag and simply gave up. Around 400 of its troops switched sides, greatly reinforcing the understrength Rwandans.

Due to the presence of at least one battalion of the DSP in Lubumbashi, the Rwandans expected a battle and thus manoeuvred one of their companies around the city, eventually blocking all the exit roads. But even the DSP company in Lubumbashi refused to fight. Instead, its troops fled to the airport to board several passenger and transport aircraft and disappeared toward Kinshasa. The RPA let them do so then marched on, leaving the AFDL to secure Lubumbashi and mop up the few pockets of resistance around the airport, mainly offered by DSP troops who had not managed to flee. According to some sources, the insurgents were actually rather busy shooting looters armed with stolen weapons from the fleeing soldiers, or were involved in rampaging through the local military base and Mobutu's residence, and setting them on fire. The only serious engagement in the entire Katanga Province occurred in the town of Kasumbalesa on the border with Zambia, where a group of FNLC fighters took over the local army

garrison and clashed with the AFDL when it tried to disarm them. Up to 20 Katangese were killed.

Elsewhere, the RPA quickly took Tshikapa, and then the diamond centre of Mbuji-Mayi – the capital of Kasai Orientale Province – that fell without a fight on 4 April, and where large enthusiastic crowds greeted the rebels. Kananga, the capital of Western Kasai Province, looted and heavily damaged by retreating FAZ troops, and Ilebo and Kikwit followed in quick succession, as did Kolwezi, said to have been "captured by vehicles previously seized in the town by a small group of infiltrated rebels".[*] With this, the economic heart of Zaire was under Rwandan and AFDL control. Most places surrendered without a shot being fired, but subsequently became scenes of chaos and pillage. The mayor of Kananga, whose brother had died in police custody only two months earlier, openly sided with the rebels, and ordered all Kanangan police and able-bodied men to brandish their swords "against the enemy" – which was now Mobutu and the FAZ. Subsequently, the town's military commander – who also sided with the Rwandans and rebels – established a reign of terror in Kananga, allowing the security forces to torture civilians and loot property without discretion.

It was also in the Kananga area that additional units of the Angolan army – at least two mechanized regiments under the command of General Paulo Lara – linked up with the AFDL forces. Well equipped with T-55 MBTs, BMP-2 IFVs, artillery and bridging equipment, they further accelerated their pace of advance. Kikwit, roughly 400km east of Kinshasa, fell on 30 April and, by 5 May, the allies reached Kenge, only 200km from the capital. Kenge became the scene of another perfidy of the Zairian military. Namely, Kinshasa deployed a battalion of the DSP, reinforced by a company-sized UNITA outfit, a few ALiR companies and a number of mercenaries of various nationalities toward Kenge, where – in their eagerness to see the AFDL arrive – some inhabitants had already destroyed all symbols of Mobutu's rule, and had prepared welcome banners for the insurgents. The combined DSP/UNITA/ALiR unit reached the town on 4 May and summarily executed an unknown number of civilians for treason. On the following day, an overextended column of Angolan and Rwandan troops and AFDL insurgents reached Kenge, only to run into an

---

★ Reyntjens, *The Great African War*, p.109

Kananga, as seen in the late 1960s. *Photo Mark Lepko Collection*

The FAA units deployed in southern Zaire during May 1997 added plenty of urgently required firepower to overstretched, thinly spread and lightly armed columns of the advancing RPA and ADFL. Here Angolan troops bring their M-46 130mm towed field gun into position outside Kenge. *Photo Albert Grandolini Collection*

they were quickly outflanked by the Angolans, who had brought bridging equipment of Russian origin with them, and were forced to withdraw again. The alliance was now within 180km of Kinshasa.

Although retreating, the DSP battalion was not yet finished. On 10 May, they blew up the Bombo River Bridge, 90km short of the capital and then prepared another ambush, fortifying the area. Once again, employing the bridging equipment brought in by the Angolans, the Rwandans deployed a battalion of 500 troops to cross the river upstream, outflanking the enemy and leaving the Guards with no choice but to fall back, this time to the Nsele River Bridge near one of the FAZ bases, only 55km west of Kinshasa. Here, the Rwandans and Angolans caught them by surprise during the night of 15/16 May, forcing the DSP back again. Not even a deployment of seven T-62 light tanks of the 1st Armoured Brigade by rail from Mbanza–Ngungu was of any help: their crews abandoned them intact.

Late on 16 May, a mixed column of around 2,000 Rwandan, Angolan and AFDL troops reached the N'Djili IAP where the last known armed clash of the war occurred. An FAZ company attempted to prevent the invaders from taking the airport and the nearby military base. According to Red Cross reports, some 200 people, including many civilians, were killed, with 52 injured. In Kinshasa, there was chaos,

ambush set in the town centre. During the course of this clash, that saw an extensive deployment of recoilless rifles, MLRS and mortars, up to 65 people – including 20 Angolan and Rwandan soldiers, but primarily civilians – were killed and 126 others injured. Thirty other civilians were executed by Zairian and UNITA troops before they retreated a few kilometres to set up another ambush outside the town. After suffering additional losses, the Angolans and Rwandans left their troops to fall back to Kenge and then regrouped while drawing the enemy into a counterattack. After running into an ambush and suffering around 100 killed, the DSP and UNITA troops fell back to the Kwango River Bridge. While occupied with looting and raping,

even though the city was largely spared a bloody fight and violence against the population (with the exception of the Binza district, where disgruntled DSP troops raped and pillaged before fleeing across the Congo River to Brazzaville). Many FAZ troops decided to defect to the AFDL, or at least cease resistance, but hardcore supporters of Mobutu went round settling scores with anybody suspected of betrayal. Before fleeing to Congo-Brazzaville, they managed to assassinate General Mahele while he was addressing the remaining DSP troops at Camp Tshatshi. The reason given was that Mahele was the one who had told Mobutu that the end was imminent and had ordered the FAZ to keep calm and cooperate with the enemy, regarding the situation as hopeless.

A Type-62 tank of the 1st Armoured Brigade FAZ during a pre-war parade in Kinshasa. Half a company of these was deployed to Nsele in May 1997, but all were abandoned intact by their crews before entering the battle. *Photo Albert Grandolini Collection*

The fate of the sole AS 332 Super Puma, one of the last helicopters delivered by Aérospatiale to Zaire, remains unclear. According to unconfirmed reports, it was burned by AFDL insurgents either in Kisangani or in Kindu. *Photo Aérospatiale*

The empty hulk of the Mi-35 '9T-HM3' as found abandoned at Gbadolite in May 1997. *Photo Angelo Matari*

The sad fate of MiG-21s delivered to Zaire in early 1997 is best described by photographs like this, showing them, only partially assembled, as they were abandoned at Gbadolite. *Photo James Moor*

Spearheaded by the 101st Battalion RPA, the AFDL insurgents, led by Jacques Malanda and followed by Angolan units, silently entered the Congolese capital without encountering any resistance, on the morning of 17 May 1997. Once the soldiers of the various FAZ units and security forces became aware of their presence, they surrendered peacefully. Some sided with the AFDL, but most were arrested and taken to N'Dolo where a large PoW camp, and collection point for arms handed over by the previous Zairian troops, had been established. The RPA/AFDL troops then began searching for former dignitaries and members of the DSP, arresting and summarily executing suspects. Between 228 and 318 bodies were collected in Kinshasa and its surrounds by the National Red Cross over the following days. Through the rest of May and during June, large numbers of public executions of former FAZ soldiers and political opponents of the AFDL – often aided by the civilian population – were carried out. In some cases, arrested persons were taken out of their prison cells or local hospitals, led to the riverside, executed and their bodies dumped into the water. Many prisoners died as a result of ill-treatment, malnutrition, unhygienic conditions and lack of medical care. This practice only stopped after fierce protests from various human rights organizations.*

* The AFDL's *kadogos* developed a strong predilection for cruel, inhuman and degrading treatment. Public floggings with the *chicotte*, a leather-thonged whip, were common practice; this usually caused massive internal bleeding and thus death. See UN Report of the Mapping Exercise, pp. 147-8.

Final act of the snarkotunities

The fall of Kinshasa did not immediately end the First Congo War. While the capital was falling, various top Zairian military officials and scattered remnants of the FAZ were fleeing across the Congo River to Brazzaville, and a large contingent of the Civil Guard withdrew in the direction of Matadi. Mobutu and his entourage fled to Gbadolite, where, officially, they began organizing resistance, but were in fact waiting to be evacuated from the country. Chaos was unavoidable, and it was under these circumstances that one of the final dramas relating to Mobutu's rule took place in Gbadolite.

As mentioned, when deciding to contract foreign mercenaries in late 1996, the Zairian government operated along two axes. The one resulted in hiring French, Belgian and Serbian contingents. The second was more promising, even though far less successful. Sometime in late October or early November 1996, Kinshasa approached the South African PMC, Executive Outcomes (EO) – renowned for its successes in Angola and Sierra Leone – inquiring whether it would be prepared to support the FAZ. The company's CO, Eeben Barlow, turned down the offer, citing his company's obligations to the Angolan government as a reason. Stability Control Agency (usually shortened to Stabilco, and registered in the Isle of Man) approached the Zairians with a tender to raise a squadron of helicopter gunships flown by experienced South African pilots, a fighting battalion of some 500 ground troops to support the FAZ in combat, and provide logistic, communication and recruitment services. After much persistence, they managed to contact General

AFDL troops at one of several points set up in Kinshasa where FAZ and DSP troops surrendered and handed over their arms.
Photo Mark Lepko Collection

Baramoto in November 1996. Initially he did little but refer Stabilco to General Nzimbi and Admiral Mayua. In mid-December, Baramoto left a few of the South African pilots recruited by Stabilco – some of them former employees of the EO – to tour the FAZA bases in order to establish the status of Zairian combat aircraft and helicopters. The pilots found enormous amounts of equipment and armament stored in different depots, but most of it was still packed in transportation containers – exactly as on delivery – and thus of little use, while much of the support equipment and electronics was missing. At N'Djili they found one C-130H – fresh from overhaul in South Africa, but already missing three engines – a single Caribou and around 20 SF 260s, all stored, in reasonable condition but not flyable.*

At Kindu, the South Africans found several SA 342 Gazelles – all taken from Rwanda – and three FAZA Pumas, all unattended and unguarded and obviously in need of maintenance. Although spending millions purchasing this equipment, training pilots, technicians and ground crews abroad, the Zairians lacked the capability to repair these aircraft and make them ready for combat. Worse yet, although spending even more money for training FAZA pilots, there was a persistent fear among top Zairian commanders that the pilots could not be trusted, that they would use the aircraft and helicopters to

defect or even launch an attack on the government. Therefore, the air force was effectively grounded.

Following this inspection, weeks lapsed without anything happening, until a new round of negotiations between Kinshasa and Stabilco was launched in early January 1997, this time with General Mahele as the Zairian representative. While Mahele was candid in admitting that his people were simply not up to the job and were in need of help, he was sceptical about Stabilco's ability to swiftly deploy a fighting force in Zaire, and would not accept its demands for upfront payments to finance the acquisition of necessary equipment and transportation for the enterprise. Although eventually accepting an operational plan proposed by the South Africans, even Mahele did next to nothing for the next six months – probably because he was busy attempting to command the FAZ during the battles for Maniema Province and Kisangani. It was only on 1 May 1997 that Stabilco's representatives were finally informed that the government had decided to award them a contract (worth between US$90 and 100 million), and that they were expected to start deploying their fighters to Gbadolite as soon as possible.

By the time Stabilco received the contract and its personnel reached Gbadolite, the aircraft and helicopters purchased for the Legion Blanc were in poor condition. No pilots were left to fly the remaining two Mi-24s and there were very few Russian technicians, and even less spare parts and fuel for them. Jastrebs were inoperable because the Serbs had deliberately sabotaged them before leaving. There were also no batteries to power up either of these. The MiG-21s arrived

---

* Venter, Al J., *Gunship Ace*, pp. 149-50. Only years later did the South Africans learn that General Baruti, CO *1 Groupement Aérien*, had sold the engines to a local trader, together with an export permit to get them out of the country. Apparently this happened to many of the FAZA's SF 260s (sold to the USA, leaving only eight in storage at N'Dolo).

unassembled (for the purpose of transportation) and were to be put together by a group of Russian technicians. For unknown reasons, but also because of the lack of the necessary oils and greases (ordered from Moscow but never delivered) this work was never completed. All the MiGs were abandoned on the tarmac of Gbadolite in partially assembled condition, with their sensitive cockpits and avionic bays left open, fully exposed to the elements.

Eventually, the South Africans decided to fly the two Mi-24s to Kinshasa, but this idea was abandoned when they learned of the fall of the capital on 15 May. The following day, Mobutu and his entourage, of around 100, arrived at Gbadolite in his presidential B707. During the early hours of 17 May 1997, they were flown out of the country on board a chartered Il-76 transport, never to return. Mobutu died in Rabat, Morocco, three months later. Left on their own, and with Rwandan and insurgent troops approaching Gbadolite, the South Africans found no other way but to escape toward the Central African Republic (CAR).

Contrary to some expectations, the RPA and AFDL approached Gbadolite in an understated fashion. Instead of doing so when their first push on this town was expected, in March and April 1996, they passed by to capture Mbandaka, a port of the Zaire River about 600km northeast of Kinshasa. Eventually, a combined column of RPA and AFDL troops approached Gbadolite on 17 May 1997. With Mobutu out of the country, what was left of the local DSP and FAZ units went berserk. They turned into a drunken, rampaging mob that systematically looted property, and killing, slugging or raping whoever crossed their path before fleeing in the direction of the CAR, together with a mass of Zairian civilians and Rwandan refugees. Gbadolite was so comprehensively destroyed that even years later all that was left of this symbol of Mobutu's rule over Congo/Zaire, were ruined villas with broken walls and swimming pools.

The rest of what was once Zaire collapsed in similar fashion. On 22 May 1997, the insurgents reached the port of Matadi without meeting any resistance and, a day later, entered the huge military base of Kitona. The last remaining FAZ units surrendered, while those DSP and Civil Guard troops that were still in the area scattered across the border into Angola. The First Congo War thus came to an end amid bloody chaos in which people were already considering and acting upon the opportunity to acquire what they could of what was left of Zaire's wealth, while their troops were either pillaging and raping, or herding the remaining Rwandan refugees and surviving DSP and FAZ officers, NCOs and soldiers.

CONCEPT PLAN OF ATTACK - BUKAVU AIRFIELD

SITUATION

1. The rebel forces in Zaire have occupied most of the major centres in the eastern part of the country and threaten to occupy the strategic town of Kisangani. Kisangani is the last major airfield in the area which will allow relatively easy counter offensive operations against the rebel forces.
2. The rebel forces have good logistic supply lines and have been able to make use of much of the arms and ammunition abandoned by retreating Government Forces. However, their supply lines are now becoming longer and it will become more difficult to replenish logistic requirements.
3. The morale of the government troops is low, as well as that of the population of Zaire. An operation is required to counter the rebel offensive, and to provide a boost to the morale of the Armed forces of Zaire and to the population as a whole.

AIM OF THIS CONCEPT PLAN

4. The aim of this concept plan is to provide various options for the occupation of Bukavu Airfield for the harassment of and to deny the supply of logistics to the rebel forces in eastern Zaire.

OPTION 1

5. <u>Phases</u>. This option is the staging of the operation from Kisangani and directly attacking Bukavu Airfield. The operation consists of the following phases:

    i. <u>Phase 1</u>. Reconnaissance of the area and Bukavu airfield by air and if the situation allows, by ground.
    ii. <u>Phase 2</u>. A helicopter assault offensive operation against rebel positions at Bukavu.
    iii. <u>Phase 3</u>. Consolidation of position at Bukavu Airfield. Landing of balance of force and logistics by fixed wing transport aircraft on Bukavu Airfield. The initiation of operations against the rebel forces and logistic bases and supply lines.
    iv. <u>Phase 4</u>. Frontal attack from Kisangani along road to Bukavu.

6. <u>Advantages</u>.

    i. Surprise.
    ii. Interdiction behind enemy lines
    iii. Deny logistic supply to the rebel forces.
    iv. Places immediate political pressure on Rwanda and Burundi.
    v. Create a divided enemy front and enemy will have to re-deploy forces to contain threat on their rear positions.
    vi. Improve morale of the Government Forces and relieve pressure on the Government politicians.
    vii. National morale will improve.

The first page of Stabilco's secret Concept Plan of Attack – Bukavu Airfield, developed by Roelf van Heerden in Kinshasa in early 1997 and provided to the Zairian government. *Roelf van Heerden, via Andrew Hudson*

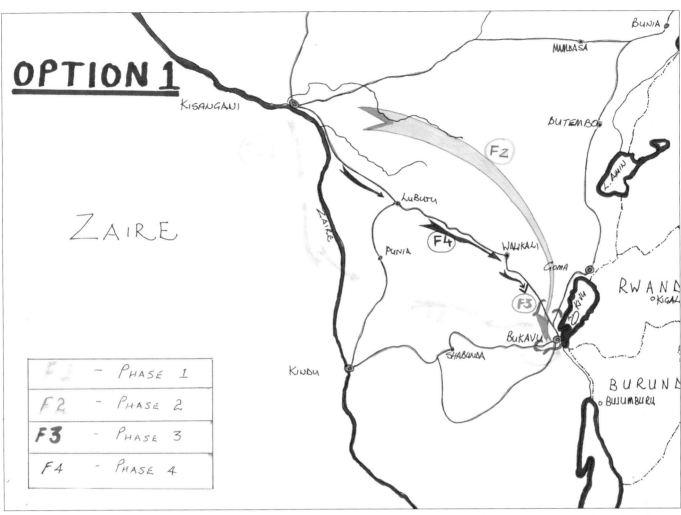

One of five options for the attack on Bukavu, as developed by Roelf van Heerden and proposed to the Zairian government, envisaged a heliborne assault operation, staged out of Kisangani, with the aim of capturing Bukavu airfield and initiating operations against the rebel forces and their logistic bases and supply lines. This plan was assessed as risky, primarily because the deployed force would have faced major difficulties with regard to logistic replenishment and, without knowledge of the direct involvement of the RPA, van Heerden also expected interference by "Rwanda and/or Burundi Forces". However, exploiting the element of surprise, it was likely to succeed and van Heerden expected not only to deny the use of Bukavu airfield to the rebels, but also place immediate political pressure on Rwanda and Burundi, create a divided enemy front, improve the morale of the FAZ and the nation and relieve pressure on the government in Kinshasa.

Detailed view of the front section of one of the MiG-21 PFMs abandoned at Gbadolite. *Photo James Moor*

The single-seater MiG-21s delivered to Zaire were of the PFM variant, actually ill suited for COIN warfare, having only one pylon under each wing and no internal cannon. Still, if deployed in an aggressive and effective manner, they could have proved a threat, not only to RPA and AFDL troops, but also to the many transport aircraft and helicopters operating on behalf of the Rwandans, hauling troops and supplies over eastern Zaire during mid-1997. *Photo James Moor*

CHAPTER FIVE:
CONCLUSION

It appears simple to describe the First Congo War as yet another ethnic conflict of the 1990s: typically massive suffering for the civilian population, low-intensity warfare between rag-tag rebel groups and widespread use of obsolete yet simple, low-technology armament thrown out with the Cold War. In fact, the most important effect of this war was a complete realignment of a number of Central African nations – including much of Sudan – from alliances with France and Belgium to ones with the USA and Israel. Indeed, although parts of the US State Department, as well as representatives *in situ*, might not have known – or did not care – what was actually going on, the USA emerged as a new, decisive power in Africa, albeit through pulling strings behind the scenes.

While there is little doubt that most of the fighting took place under relatively simple – not to mention primitive – circumstances, certain age-old principles of warfare were again confirmed, but so were specific new patterns of African warfare of the 1990s. For example, the fate of Rwandan Hutu refugees played into the strategy of major protagonists in Kigali and their foreign supporters. When survivors of spontaneous repatriation fled deeper into Zaire, the RPA – followed by the AFDL – launched a merciless hunt that ultimately collapsed the government in Kinshasa. In the process of the invasion the Rwandans made good use of the media to cover up their actual intentions and capabilities, but also completely dehumanized their enemy – not only with the aim of motivating their own fighters, but also to reach their security and political objectives, as well as a favourable economic situation. Therefore, this conflict – which subsequently became known as the First Congo War – was far more than an economic insurgency as is sometimes stated. Unlike many other contemporary African wars, it was not border conflict, but more of a proxy war and a substitute battlefield where the value of propaganda of the dead and the utilization of brutality became as omnipresent as in Liberia or Sierra Leone.

Operational considerations

The history of modern warfare in Africa saw a number of countries facing foreign invasion well before the mid-1990s. With one exception (the war between Tanzania and Uganda of 1978–79), never before did any African country face, as its adversary, another African nation in possession of a military capability comparable with that which Rwanda, Uganda and Angola deployed in Zaire from 1996. It had also not previously occurred that a conflict had resulted in the complete defeat of one of the participating nations. Part of the reason for this lies in Zaire becoming a default battlefield where several major developments at operational and tactical levels were put to their ultimate tests.

Militarily, perhaps the most important lesson of this war was the difference in the quality of the officer corps of two major belligerents, Rwanda and Zaire. Like in so many other countries in Africa, the FAZ officer corps was completely unprofessional, to the degree where the pursuit of a military career was merely seen as a path to economic gain and political influence, and not imbued with the patriotism of serving one's country. By comparison, the RPA managed to field a highly professional and disciplined officer corps, which during the First Congo War provided it with several masterpieces of military craft in terms of organization, logistics, command of combat operations, economy of force, and on-the-spot improvisation.

Secondly, although the involved armies and insurgencies were trained and equipped with the help of arms and equipment from very different sources, both sides' weapons were close to obsolete and virtually inoperable; they also wore uniforms that were difficult to distinguish between. While this made clear identification of forces on the battlefield problematic, it also enabled them to disappear easily into the bush and reappear unexpectedly somewhere else, or even change sides.

The use of foreign, primarily Western, mercenary forces was certainly nothing new, but in this theatre, at this time, these forces were of a wholly different quality. Years before, relatively small mercenary forces were deployed to reach various combat-related objectives. Time and again, some of them proved able to topple governments or at least change the flow of conflict. The First Congo War saw the deployment of one such force in this manner, and then another rendering itself perfectly ineffective. Carefully hidden from the public, and no matter how influential to the outcome, the involvement of the majority of the foreign mercenaries mostly remained limited to providing advice and, primarily, logistic support.

The use of civilian transport aircraft to provide logistic support was nothing new – whether in Africa or elsewhere. However, the scope and dimension of this development was unsurpassed, spanning intercontinental distances. This aspect of the First Congo War was to further intensify during following years, and would be replicated in future African wars.

Studying the First Congo War of 1996–97 it is always surprising how easily the Rwandans and the AFDL conquered most of Zaire and toppled Mobutu's government. Throughout much of this conflict they were preoccupied with the pursuit of Hutu refugees and delivering supplies to their advancing units, than fighting the FAZ. Regardless of how often US sources use the word 'visionary' to describe top Rwandan military commanders, primarily Kagame and Kabarebe, and irrespective of the sound tactics employed by the RPA, it remains doubtful that Kigali planned to march on Kinshasa from the outset. Even in light of all the aid Rwanda received from the US, all the available information indicates that the march on Kinshasa was a development of the conflict – based on the domino effect caused by the first series of Zairian defeats – rather than original intent. By the time the RPA were approaching Kisangani, it had become the norm that the FAZ would panic, loot and then flee to the next large town, where the entire process would be repeated as soon as the Rwandans appeared. The situation developed to such an extent that the AFDL leaders would often announce they were about to attack a particular target, or that they had captured it before this had actually happened, which was enough for the FAZ to flee. This success bred confidence and this confidence broadened their horizons. The

Rwandans suddenly became aware of the fact that none of Mobutu's allies would save him, and that they could defeat the Zairian military with relative ease and install what they were hoping would become a puppet government in Kinshasa. Furthermore, although regularly ignored outright by most foreign observers, it should not be forgotten that the rapid conclusion of the conflict became possible only because of the Angolan intervention. The FAA contingent not only played a crucial role in specific operations, but resulted directly in a rapid end to the war.

Certainly, one of the important reasons for Mobutu's defeat was the complete incompetence of his government and military; the latter in particular was a hollow shell and was clearly outmatched. Nevertheless, there is still no rational explanation for the failure of the FAZ to tackle the rebellion, except that Zairian generals – concentrating on Kabila and his lack of military capabilities – never seriously considered the possibility of Rwandan involvement, nor studied the development of the RPA during 1994–96. Therefore, they concluded that Kabila's *kadogos* did not present a serious threat, and thus never took the situation seriously enough until it was too late. At least as important is that many Zairian generals simply did not care. While their isolated units were fighting for survival, they continued enjoying their corrupt lives in Kinshasa. By 1996, the Zairian military was such a quagmire of corruption and internal struggles, that there was no chance the FAZ or the FAZA could ever bring their theoretically superior firepower to bear. The FAZA was to all intents and purposes non-operational and thus could not support the army. Nearly all the army's operational artillery was lost early in the war, while mortar batteries were redundant for lack of trained personnel. The FAZ armour – which could have wreaked havoc on the lightly armed RPA and AFDL – never even appeared on the battlefield. Instead, most of the fighting was done by some of most disorganized and demoralized units of the Zairian army.

How deep the lingering hope that France would eventually save Mobutu, and that the First Congo War was as much of a disaster for Paris, are matters of considerable debate. Foremost, Mobutu and his top military and political commanders never saw the danger coming, then ignored it for far too long and finally did next to nothing to challenge it. Furthermore, Paris had almost certainly underestimated US and Rwandan involvement – but only in as much as it had already underestimated the unexpectedly negative consequences of its own, highly controversial involvement in the civil war in Rwanda. After such a disgrace, there was no chance for the French to get involved in Zaire as well, even more so because Paris actually knew that Mobutu's time had come.

The solution found in this situation was one of a quick fix: hiring mercenaries. Not only in theory, but as proven in practice dozens of times before, a few hundred combat-tested Europeans, with a few fighter jets and helicopter gunships should have been enough not only to stem, but defeat outright the insurgency – provided the AFDL was just another typical African insurgent group that came into being on its own and lacked any kind of foreign support. However, the insurgency was not limited to the AFDL. On the contrary, the RPA played a crucial role in the war, which meant that the FAZ and the foreign mercenaries went into battle against a combat-tested, well-organized, well-trained and expertly-led military force. This is something the Europeans were simply not ready for. After their defeat, which greatly encouraged the Rwandans and insurgents, Mobutu's control of Zaire imploded.

The right profile of the third MiG-21PFM abandoned at Gbadolite. Behind it can be seen the front section of the sole MiG-21 UM two-seater conversion trainer. *Photo Angelo Matari*

Although some foreign observers – including Lieutenant-Colonel Richard Orth, the US defence attaché in Kigali during the war – subsequently insisted that the Rwandans played a rather modest role, saying that they deployed only "two or three mobile light battalion-sized formations" and that their main contribution was in form of providing combat-tested veteran officers to lead the insurgents, the information available contradicts this. The AFDL was assembled, organized, trained, equipped and run by Rwanda and its foreign supporters. Not only the AFDL's military wing, but also its political leaders were under tight RPA control during the war and for several months afterward. All the major operations were undertaken by the RPA, which deployed its best units for the purpose. Even Kagame – who also insisted that most of the guerrilla fighters were Zairians (which might have been true later in the war when the AFDL's ranks increased dramatically following the fall of Kisangani and Lubumbashi) – admitted that the insurgency was not prepared to carry the war to its conclusion on its own, that it was led and directed by Rwandan officers, that key units belonged to his forces, that these fought all the crucial, hard-won battles and that RPA units were directly involved in the capture of all the major cities that fell to the insurgents, from Bukavu and Goma, to Kisangani, Lubumbashi, Kenge and Kinshasa. Because of this, it is clear that foreign support for the AFDL and thus Rwanda was decisive in the outcome of this war. Superior discipline, training, logistic support and leadership of the field forces enabled the RPA to overcome its own challenges, the weaknesses of the insurgents it was propping up, and those of the FAZ. The weight of this support was simply overwhelming.

Rwandan *Rezzou*

Regardless how well financed, organized and supported the RPA and the AFDL were, they could still not have succeeded where so many earlier insurgencies in Congo/Zaire had failed, namely in advancing rapidly and conquering huge swaths of territory and ultimately toppling the government in Kinshasa, without one very important detail: the RPA's very advanced tactical methods were tailored to local conditions. While based on traditional African-style warfare, these methods involved elements of special forces and unconventional warfare tactics, carefully adapted for simple application under local circumstances.

RPA offensive operations usually followed a relatively simple formula, along which every attack was to aim for the heart of the defender and quickly bring it down. At operational level, the preferable target was the seat of the enemy government, or at the very least, the high command of Mobutu's military. On a tactical level, local military or political headquarters was the primary target. This formula did not require the deployed force to be especially capable, numerically superior or in possession of superior firepower, as it was not seeking to breach enemy front lines or defeat units in a classic, complex, set-piece battle in which enemy units are physically destroyed. Instead, the attacking force looked to infiltrate enemy positions and collapse resistance by attacking their commanders. This made it unnecessary for the involved force to concentrate before going into action. On the contrary, concentrations of forces in front of enemy positions would have made enemy detection through reconnaissance or intelligence easy. Instead, the force would disperse in front of the enemy, infiltrate their positions, penetrate deep behind their lines, reassemble and regroup at a predetermined time and place, and then deliver the main blow, preferably causing the enemy to collapse from within. Thus the deployed force only needed to be strong enough,

with correspondingly sufficient firepower, to quickly neutralize the guards protecting the enemy centre of power.

What is little known is that this method of fighting a war, sometimes called the Rwandan Infiltration or *Rezzou* (which translates roughly to 'raiding party' in English), was almost certainly developed during the course of the war by succeeding RPA commanders who adopted US military tactics of the late 1980s and early 1990s and had already been thoroughly tested in Angola, Chad and Rwanda. The experiences in Chad had contributed predominantly in proving the usability of the *rezzou* concept with operational as well as tactical planning. There the motorized columns of Toyota pickup trucks, led by the US- and French-trained officer Idriss Déby, proved capable of penetrating even heavily protected Libyan bases, and defeating mechanized forces during the so-called Toyota War. Déby subsequently fell into disfavour with his government, but in November 1990 he emerged from a base in Sudan to unleash a decisive attack on N'Djamena. Outmanoeuvring forward army units and avoiding large-scale battles, columns of his fighters advanced over 800km in less than

An infiltration uses covert movement of forces through enemy lines to attack positions in the enemy rear

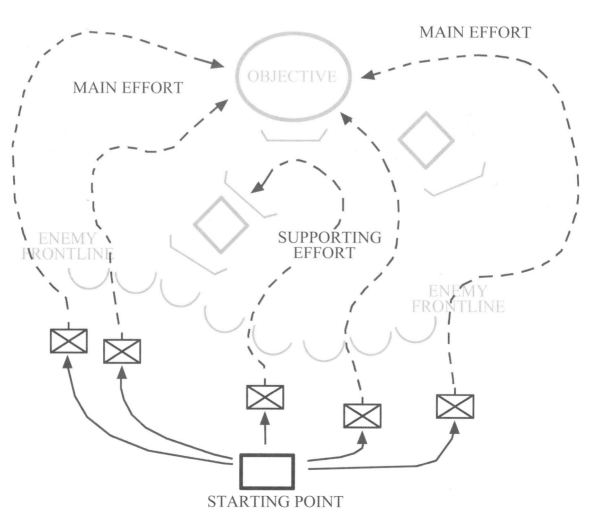

The basic principles of infiltration tactics

three weeks, and, in early December 1990, captured the presidential palace in the Chadian capital, toppling the government in the process. This blow came so suddenly that many foreign observers suspected some kind of a coup d'état from within.

Similarly, when the RPA launched its advance on Kigali in October 1990, the deployed force consisted of only 50 fighters. Yes, these were reinforced by 600 and then a further 3,000 within the following days and weeks. But, due to the speed of this execution and the element of surprise, these 50 could easily have proven sufficient to bring down the government in Kigali were it not for the sizeable French and Zairian defence reinforcements.

Obviously, speed in an operation of this nature, and the use of natural features and terrain to conceal a deployment are crucial. The force should preferably be spread thinly in front of enemy positions, infiltrate them, reassemble behind their lines and hit the actual target well before the defenders recognize their presence or can reinforce the protection of their centre of power or military headquarters. Whenever the attacking force failed to do so, when it failed to destroy its target with the first blow, or when it was recognized too early or faced a well-trained opponent who had established a strong defensive position, it usually rapidly ran out of ammunition and supplies, succumbing to the defender's firepower.

As strange as it might sound, with its rugged terrain, dense vegetation and poor land communications, and despite its sheer size, Zaire was a perfect battlefield for this method of fighting. The Rwandans could fully exploit the heat, humidity and thick vegetation surrounding most populous centres to deploy their troops wearing civilian clothes and carrying disassembled weapons in order to infiltrate enemy positions. Their experience from the wars in Uganda and Rwanda, and their capability and preparedness to improvise, but also the inertia and poor communications of their opponents, helped them immensely.

Consequences of the First Congo War

The most important consequence of the First Congo War was that it marked the end of the beginning of a process that can only be described as the strategic realignment of nearly the entire Central African region. The alliance between the Zairian AFDL, the RPA and Museveni's Uganda, plus the USA and, via the USA and Uganda, the alignment with the insurgents of the Sudanese People's Liberation Army in southern Sudan, marked a significant change in the political makeup of the entire area. This strategic realignment resulted in the establishment of governments with strong ties to the USA and Israel, instead of France and Belgium, as during earlier times.

However, while the general feeling outside Zaire, after the fall of Kinshasa, was that the chaos of the last few years of Mobutu's reign might finally end, and that the alliance of relatively new revolutionary governments in this part of Africa would likely portend well for future stability of the entire area, the situation subsequently developed in a diametrically opposite direction. First and foremost, the new order in Zaire, Rwanda and Uganda did little to implement significant social and economic changes, resulting in no political liberation. On the contrary, it was succeeded by a sharp decline, particularly in regard to human rights and the overall state of the economy.

Laurent Kabila, the supposed liberator, soon proved to be far worse than Mobutu and his entire clique had ever been. Although forming a government dominated by various AFDL leaders, promising democratic elections and renaming Zaire to the Democratic Republic of Congo (DRC) on 23 May 1997, he showed little interest in power-sharing and began installing members of his family in crucial economic and political positions almost immediately. After most of the principal opposition parties announced that they did not recognize Kabila's government, he issued a law strictly curtailing their activities and ordered a brutal crackdown on their leaders and activists. Meanwhile, the RPA and AFDL continued their merciless hunt for Rwandan refugees. They continued tracking, herding and killing them all over the Congo. What was left of the ALiR inside the country were small groups of confused fighters scattered anywhere between the jungles of the Kivus and the dense forests of the Equateur Province, but many of them continued fighting. By June 1997, they had already sided with several Mayi-Mayi militias to launch an uprising against the Rwandans, Banyamasasi and Banyamulenge. Meanwhile, even the Angolan army became involved in violence against Congolese civilians. Their government ordered them to launch a crackdown against Angolan refugees from the Cabinda enclave in the Bas-Congo Province – many of whom had fought against Luanda in the 1980s. Exactly how many people lost their lives in the resultant atrocities is unlikely to ever come to light.

Although South Africa, and then Angola, Rwanda, Burundi, Libya and Zimbabwe recognized the new government in Kinshasa, Kabila was soon isolated by most Western powers. Some turned against him because of massive human rights violations and others because he did not keep a single promise in regard to his commercial ties to business establishments in Washington and elsewhere. Furthermore, when he began replacing Rwandan officers within the ranks of the newly established military with members of his family and tribe, Kabila found himself at odds even with his most important ally, the government in Kigali – the very same people who had brought him to power – and this to the extent where the Rwandans began organizing political and military opposition against him. Thus, the new strongman in Kinshasa sowed the seeds of a new, even larger and more brutal conflict almost as soon as the First Congo War ended.

Bibliography

The First and Second Congo Wars took place from 1996–97 and 1998–2003 respectively and remain highly pertinent in terms of Central Africa's modern history. Neither of the two conflicts changed anything in regard to human rights, press freedom or access to official documentation in the relevant countries. On the contrary, many participants have meanwhile been forced to leave their homelands, rightly concerned about their safety, and finding no other solution but to request asylum in the European Union. It is because of this, that while much of the material compiled during the preparation of this publication is based on interviews with first-hand participants of the Congo Wars, these were obtained on the basis of absolute anonymity. Other participants became involved in the conflicts through their active military service, or employment with various foreign air freight companies or private military companies. While some of them have since retired, their freedom to speak openly remains limited. On the other hand, all the US, Rwandan, Ugandan and some British officials contacted in the research stages of this publication refused to offer any commentary, citing "matters of national security" and "official secrets" as reasons for their silence. Nevertheless, all contributions have proved precious and enabled the author to cross-examine the following publications (as well as those mentioned in footnotes), consulted during the writing of this book.

Barlow, Eeben, *Executive Outcomes: Against all Odds*, , Galago Alberton, 1999

Brent, W., *African Air Forces*, Freeworld, Nelspruit, 1999

Bugakov, I.S.; Ivanov, B.V.; Kartashev, V.B.; Laverntev, A.P.; Ligav, V.A. & Pashoko, V.A., *Kazan Helicopters: Flight Goes On*, Vertolet Publisher & Kazan Helicopters, 2001

Cochrane, J. & Elliott, S., *Military Aircraft Insignia of the World*, Airlife Publishing, Shrewsbury, 1998

Cooper, T., 'Darfur: Krieg der Antonow Bomber', *Fliegerrevue Extra* magazine, Issue 20 March 2008, Germany, 2008

Cooper, T., 'Tschad: Hintergründe', script for briefing on situation in Chad, delivered to the Offiziersgesellschaft Wien, 3 April 2008, Austria, 2008

Cooper, T., '45 Years of Wars and Insurgencies in Chad', *Truppendienst* magazine, Vol. 6/2009, Austria, 2009

Cooper, T., Weinert P., Hinz F. & Lepko M., *African MiGs, MiGs and Sukhois in Service in Sub-Saharan Africa, Volume 1: Angola to Ivory Coast*, Harpia Publishing, Vienna, 2010

Cooper, T., Weinert P., Hinz F. & Lepko M., *African MiGs, MiGs and Sukhois in Service in Sub-Saharan Africa, Volume 2: Madagascar to Zimbabwe*, Harpia Publishing, Vienna, 2011

Dupuy, T.N. (Col, US Army, ret.), & Blanchard W. (Col, US Army, ret.) *The Almanac of World Military Power* (Dunn Loring/ T.N. Dupuy Ass/Arthur Barker Ltd., London, 1972

Flintham, V., *Air Wars and Aircraft: A Detailed Record of Air Combat 1945 to the Present*, Arms & Armour Press, London, 1989

Fruchart, D., *United Nations Arms Embargoes: Their Impact on Arms Flows and Target Behaviour, Case Study: Rwanda, 1994-Present*, SIPRI, 2007

Garrett, N., *The Extractive Industries Transparency Initiative & Artisanal and Small-Scale Mining, Preliminary Observations from the Democratic Republic of the Congo*, Extractive Industries Transparency Initiative

Gleijeses, P., *Conflicting Missions: Havana, Washington, and Africa, 1959–1976*, The University of North Carolina Press, Chapel Hill, 2002

Green, W. & Fricker, J., *The Air Forces of the World: Their History, Development and Present Strength*, MacDonald & Co, London 1958

Gribbin, R., *In the Aftermath of Genocide: The US Role in Rwanda*, Universe, New York, 2005

Hammond, Dr. P., *Holocaust in Rwanda*, Frontline Fellowship, Newlands, 1996

Hermann, D., *Krieg, Ökonomie und Politik in Afrika: Eine Fallstudie am Beispiel der Demokratischen Republik Kongo*, Books on Demand GmbH/GRIN Verlag, Norderstedt, 2007

Huertas, S. M., *Dassault-Breguet Mirage III/5*, Osprey, London, 1990

Kennes, E., *The Democratic Republic of the Congo: Strucures of Greed, Networks of Need, Rethinking the Economics of War*, Woodrow Wilson Center, Washington, 2005

Laffin, J., *The World in Conflict; Contemporary Warfare Described and Analysed, War Annual 7*, Brassey's, London, 1996

Madsen, W., *Genocide and Covert Operations in Africa, 1993–1999*, African Studies, Edwin Mellen Pr, May 1999

Montague, D., 'Stolen goods: coltan and conflict in the Democratic Republic of Congo', *SAIS Review, Winter/Spring 2002*, John Hopkins University Press, Baltimore, 2002

Morgan, DR Congo's '$24 trillion fortune', *African Business*, February 2009

Newdick, T. & Cooper, T., *Modern Military Airpower, 1990–Present* Amber Books, London, 2010

Nzongola-Ntalaja, Georges, *Congo: From Leopold to Kabila: A People's History*, London, Zed Books, London

Prunier, G., *Africa's World War: Congo, the Rwandan Genocide, and the Making of a Continental Catastrophe*, Oxford University Press, London, 2009

Snow, 'The War that did not make the Headlines: Over Five Million Dead in Congo?' Global Research, 31 January 2008

Storaro, F., *1964–1984, Vent' Anni di Aeronautica Militare: Missione Africa*, Istituto Bibliografico Napoleone, Rome, 2010

Sonck, J. P & Despas, D., 'L'Aviation Katangaise', *Avions* magazine, Vols. 34–36 , 1996

Sonck, J. P., 'MB 326 Sous Le Ciel Zairois', *Jets* magazine, Vol. 10, 1996

Sonck, J. P., 'La Force Aérienne Congolaise', *Jets* magazine, volumes 32–34, 1998

Sonck, J. P., 'Echec aux Simba', *Avions* magazine, Vols, 97, 131 & 138, 2001 & 2004

Sonck, J. P., 'La Force Aérienne Congolaise', *Contact* magazine, Vols. 39 & 40, 2005

Strizek, H., *Clinton Am Kivu-See: Die Geschichte Einer Afrikanischen Katastrophe*, Peter Lang GmbH, Frankfurt am Main, 2011

Tanks of the World: Taschenbuch der Panzer (Koblenz, Bernard & Graefe Verlag, 1990

Thompson, Sir R. (ed.), *War in Peace: An Analysis of Warfare since 1945*, Orbis, London, 1981

Thorn, W. G., 'Congo-Zaire's 1996–1997 Civil War in the Context of Evolving Patterns of Military Conflict in Africa in the Era of Independence', *The Journal of Conflict Studies*, Vol. XIX, No. 2, 1999

Turner, J. W., *Continent Ablaze: The Insurgency Wars in Africa 1960 to the Present*, Arms & Armour Press, London, 1998

Turner, T., *The Congo Wars: Conflict, Myth and Reality*, Zed Books, London, 2007

United Nations, 'Report of the panel of experts on the illegal exploitation of natural resources and other forms of wealth of the Democratic Republic of the Congo', 12 April 2001

United Nations High Commission on Human Rights, 'Report of the Mapping Exercise documenting the most serious violations of human rights and international humanitarian law committed within the territory of the Democratic Republic of the Congo between March 1993 and June 2003', August 2010

Willis D. (ed.), *Aerospace Encyclopaedia of World Air Forces*, Aerospace Publishing, London, 1999

World Defence Almanac, *Military Technology* magazine, Vols. 1/91, 1/93, 1/95, 1/97, 1/98 & 1/03

Venter, A. J., *War Dog: Fighting Other People's Wars, the Modern Mercenary in Combat*, Casemate, Havertown, 2006

Venter, A. J., *Gunship Ace: The Wars of Neall Ellis, Helicopter Pilot and Mercenary*, Casemate, Havertown, 2011

Aviation News magazine (UK), various volumes, 1999–2003

Bulletin from The Office of Foreign Assets Control, Department of the Treasury USA, 26 April 2005

'Soldiers Without Borders: Crisis in Central Africa', Hearing Before the Committee on International Relations, US Congress, 5 November 1997

Acknowledgments

This book is a result of cooperation with a number of individuals from around the continent of Africa who generously provided background and insider knowledge, information and expertise. There is little doubt that this book would have been impossible without their kind help and I would like to express my special gratitude to every one of them.

Those I am at liberty to publicly thank include: Guido Potters from the Netherlands, Albert Grandolini and Jacques Guillem from France, Pit Weinert from Germany, Jean-Pierre Sonck from Belgium, Sander Peters from the Netherlands, Andrew Hudson from South Africa, Mark Lepko and Tom Long from the USA.

Many others provided invaluable support, primarily through offering their personal photographs, and for this I would like to thank, among others, Michel Bonnardeaux, Jan Laporte and Richard Vandervord.

I would also like to extend my thanks to my wife, who accompanied me through a period of intensive work, at all times providing the support I needed to complete my research and finally put pen to paper.

Tom Cooper, from Austria, is a military-aviation journalist and historian. Following a career in a worldwide transportation business – where, during his extensive travels in Europe and the Middle East, he established excellent contacts with many first-hand sources – he moved into writing. An earlier fascination with post-Second World War military aviation has narrowed to focus on smaller air forces and conflicts, about which he has collected extensive archives of material. Concentrating primarily on air warfare, which has previously received scant attention, he specializes in investigative research on little-known African and Arab air forces, as well as the Iranian Air Force. Cooper has published 14 books – including the unique 'African MiGs' series, which examines the deployment and service history of MiG and Sukhoi jet fighters in 23 sub-Saharan African air forces – as well as over 200 articles on related topics, providing a window into a number of previously unexamined yet fascinating conflicts and relevant developments. *Great Lakes Holocaust: The First Congo War, 1996–1997* and *Great Lakes Conflagration: The Second Congo War, 1998–2003* are his first offerings to the Africa@War series.